Master The Miracles of the Quran

In 10 days

Suhaib Sirajudin

Shield Crest

ISBN   978-1-910176-26-9

MMXV

A CIP catalogue record for this book
is available from the British Library

Published by
ShieldCrest
Aylesbury, Buckinghamshire,
HP22 5RR   England
www.shieldcrest.co.uk
Tel: +44 (0)333 8000 890

Glossary

Hadith	Saying of the Prophet ﷺ
Halaal	Lawful
Haraam	Unlawful
Iman	Faith
Jinns	Invisible creatures created from fire
ka'abah	House of Allah, situated in Mecca
Maqa mat Al Hariree	Name of a book
Muqatta'at	Unique combination of letters
Non-mahram	Someone who you can marry, someone who you should cover yourself in front of
Ruku	Part
Seerah	Biography of Prophet ﷺ
Surahs	Chapters
Tashdeed	Vowel sign
Tawaaf	Circumambulation of the Ka'bah seven times
Umrah	Optional pilgrimage that can be performed anytime of the year

Overview of the Contents

Table of Contents

About This Book

This book teaches you about the many miracles of the Quran. By the time you have completed it, you will be thoroughly acquainted with the different types of miracles in the Quran.

Who Should Read This Book?

This book is intended for people who want to be fully informed as to the miraculous nature of the Quran. We know that the Quran itself is the miracle of miracles, but the question is, what is it about this book that makes it miraculous? If you want to know the answer to this question then this book is for you. By the end of the course you will have examined and pondered over many of the wonderful miracles contained in the Quran.

What if you have no knowledge of the Arabic language? Fear not. This book assumes no understanding of the Arabic language. However, if you do know a little Arabic then this course will be a little easier for you.

How The Book Is Structured?

This book is designed to be read and absorbed over the course of two weeks. During each week, you will read five chapters that explain to you various miracles contained in the Quran.

How The Content Is Organized?

Master the Miracles of the Quran in 10 Days covers the different types of miracles in the Quran in 10 days, divided into two separate working weeks, therefore, Saturdays and Sundays are excluded. The miracles are categorised according to type and each week broadly covers a specific category as exemplified in the Quran.

In the first week, you will learn about the miracles related to the language of the Quran, the style, the eloquence, the choice of words and the way the Quran describes a scene.

- Day 1 is the basic introduction: What is a miracle? What is the purpose of a miracle? You will also learn about the difference between the miracles of the Quran and the miracles demonstrated by other Prophets.

- On Day 2, you will be enlightened on how the Quran impacted on the disbelievers, especially those who were the enemies of Islam. Allah challenges anyone to bring forward something similar to the Quran.

- On Day 3, you will go into detail about the Quran's linguistic style and come to know how Allah uses precisely the right words in the right places.

- Day 4, explains why Allah reverses the order in certain verses and you will also learn about the unique conciseness of speech in the Quran.

- Day 5 is about the scenes that Allah describes for us in the Quran.

Week 2 is dedicated to the scientific miracles in the Quran:

- Day 6, is about the scientific miracles in the universe.

- On Day 7, you will study scientific miracles in the universe and on the Earth as mentioned in the Quran.

- On Day 8, you will study in greater detail the scientific miracles on the Earth as mentioned in the Quran.

- On Day 9, you will learn about the miracles of the human body as mentioned in the Quran.

- Day 10 is about other miracles the Quran mentions: Miracle of numbers, miracle of environment, miracle of laws and miracle of logic.

Each chapter concludes with a series of questions about that day's subject matter by which you are prompted to revisit the material covered in order to identify what you have learned.

WEEK

AT A GLANCE

1
2
3
4
5

- An introduction to the Miracles of the Quran
- Effect of the Quran on the disbelievers and the Challenge of the Quran
- Miracle of the Eloquence of the Quran
- Miracle of the Structure of Sentences in the Quran
- Miracles of the Scenes in the Quran

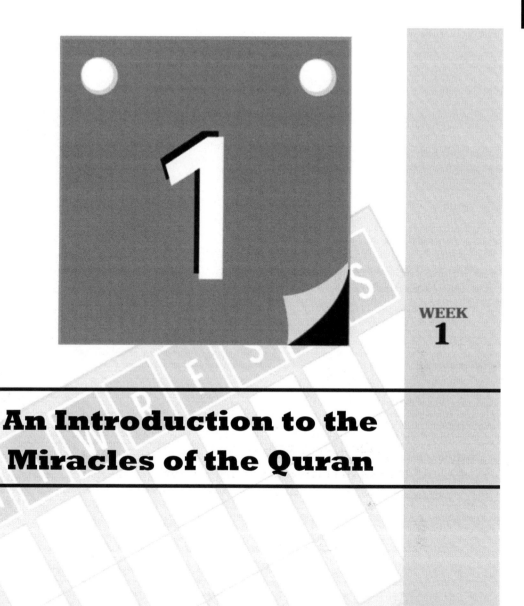

An Introduction to the Miracles of the Quran

DAY 1

Introduction to the Miracles of the Quran

Welcome to *Master the Miracles of the Quran in 10 Days!* Starting today, over the next two weeks you will learn about the miracles mentioned in the Quran and as you encounter these miracles you will be amazed, and wonder how it is that you have managed to remain unaware for so long of these amazing phenomena in the Quran. This will increase your Iman (faith) and bring you closer to Allah.

That's the overall goal for the next 10 days. Today, the goal is an introduction to this book and you'll learn the following:

- What is a miracle?
- The difference between the miracle of the Quran and the miracles of other Prophets;
- The effect of the Quran on the non-believers at the time it was being revealed to Muhammad ﷺ.
- Proof that Muhammad ﷺ is not the author of the Quran;

You may be asking yourself, why should I study the miracles of the Quran? If you are a not yet Muslim, then these miracles will serve as evidence that for a book to have such miraculous qualities, it can only have come from God. If such a book is from God then that book requires you to follow it and act upon. However, if you are already a Muslim then you should yet study the Miracles of the Quran for the following reasons:

The first reason why you should study the Miracles of the Quran is to strengthen your Iman (faith). Prophet Ibrahim ﷺ once asked Allah, "My lord, show me how you give life to the dead." Allah replied, "Do you not have Iman?" So, Ibrahim ﷺ replied, "Yes, I do have Iman, but I want peace of mind, I want my heart to be at peace."

Ibrahim ﷺ is one of those Prophets of Allah whose Iman is praised in the Quran. Allah praises his Iman as follows:

$$إِنَّ إِبْرَاهِيمَ كَانَ أُمَّةً قَانِتًا لِلَّهِ حَنِيفًا وَلَمْ يَكُ مِنَ الْمُشْرِكِينَ$$

Ibrahim was indeed a model devoutly obedient to Allah (and) true in faith and he was not of the idolaters. (Quran 16:120)

2

So, Allah praises Ibrahim's ﷺ Iman in the Quran, but yet, when Allah asks Ibrahim ﷺ whether he believed in Him giving life to the dead or not, he replies that he is only asking because he wants peace of mind. Now, I am asking you a simple question that when your Iman is not praised in the Quran, then how much more do you think you need to satisfy your heart? How much more do you think you need that peace of mind? So this is the first reason why you should study the miracles of the Quran; in order to get peace of mind and satisfy your heart.

The second reason why you should study the miracles of the Quran is to appreciate the greatness of the Quran. When I came across these miracles, I was amazed and astonished by them. In fact, I said to myself, "I have lived all this time without knowing about these extraordinary attributes of the Quran." I regret that I was unaware of these wonders. After this study, the next time you hold a Quran in your hands, you will not just feel that you are holding a book, but that you are holding an actual miracle of Allah. I want to share with you these miracles and I want you to be aware of these miracles, so that you will too realize the greatness of this book.

Most of us read the Quran to try and finish the pages, and the chapters. For many of us the aim is to complete the Quran by recitation, without pondering over the verses. I feel that after studying these miracles, you will change the way you recite this miraculous book. After studying these miracles I hope that the next time you recite the Quran you will read a verse, pause, reflect, ponder over the verse, and then go to the next verse. You will never again read the Quran the way you used to before you knew about the miracles in the Quran.

Quran is a book that when you read it, it demands you to ponder over it. It expects you to reflect upon each verse that you recite. Allah says:

كِتَابٌ أَنْزَلْنَاهُ إِلَيْكَ مُبَارَكٌ لِيَدَّبَّرُوا آيَاتِهِ وَلِيَتَذَكَّرَ أُولُو الْأَلْبَابِ

(Here is) a Book that We have sent down unto thee, full of blessings, that they may meditate on its Signs, and that men of understanding may receive admonition. (Quran 38:29)

أَفَلَا يَتَدَبَّرُونَ الْقُرْآنَ أَمْ عَلَىٰ قُلُوبٍ أَقْفَالُهَا

Do they not then earnestly seek to understand the Quran, or are their hearts locked up by them? (Quran 47:24)

These verses encourage you not to merely recite the Quran, but to ponder and reflect on each verse.

وَهَٰذَا كِتَابٌ أَنْزَلْنَاهُ مُبَارَكٌ فَاتَّبِعُوهُ

And this is a Book that We have revealed as a blessing, so follow it. (Quran 6:155)

This verse also shows you that when you read the Quran pondering and reflecting, then blessings will descend. The more you ponder over and reflect on the verses of the Quran, the more blessings will descend upon you.

Description of the Quran

The best description of the Quran is given by Allah and by the Quran itself. Allah calls the Quran a (بُرْهَان – convincing proof). Allah says:

يَا أَيُّهَا النَّاسُ قَدْ جَاءَكُمْ بُرْهَانٌ مِنْ رَبِّكُمْ

O mankind! Verily there hath come to you a convincing proof from your Lord: (Quran 4:174)

Allah calls the Quran (موعظة – admonition), (شفاء – cure), (هادي – book which guides), (نور – light), (مبارك – blessing). All these descriptions of the Quran are unique to the Quran and no other book deserves these titles except for the Quran.

When we further read the Hadith, we find an amazing description of the Quran given by the Prophet ﷺ

عن علي قال : سمعت رسول الله صلى الله عليه وسلم يقول سَتَكُونُ فِتَنٌ قُلْتُ وَمَا الْمَخْرَجُ مِنْهَا: قال كتاب الله فيه خبر ما قبلكم ونبأ ما بعدكم وحكم ما بينكم ، هو الفصل ليس بالهزل ، هو الذي لا تزيغ به الأهواء ، ولا يشبع منه العلماء ، ولا يخلق عن كثرة رد ، ولا تنقضي عجائبه ، هو الذي من تركه من جبار قصمه الله ، ومن ابتغى الهدى في غيره أضله

الله ، هو حبل الله المتين وهو الذكر الحكيم ، وهو الصراط المستقيم ، هو الذي من عمل به

إلى صراط مستقيم (رواه الترمذي)

It was narrated by Ali ؓ that the Messenger of Allah ﷺ said, "Indeed there will be a *fitnah* (trial)." "What is the way out of it, O Messenger of Allah?" I asked. He said: "Allah's Book. In it is news for what happened before you, and information about what comes after you, and judgement for what happens among you. It is the Criterion without jest. It is the Book that whims and desires cannot distort. Scholars cannot have enough of it. It never becomes dull from reciting it too much, and its wonders never end. Whoever among the oppressive abandons it, Allah crushes him, and whoever seeks guidance from other than it, then Allah leaves him to stray. It is the firm rope of Allah, it is the wise reminder, and it is the straight path. Whoever acts according to it he is rewarded; whoever judges by it has judged justly; and whoever calls to it, is guided to the straight path" (Tirmidhi: 2906)

Although this Hadith is weak, it nevertheless demonstrates the specific qualities and merits of the Quran. What other book in the world holds these qualities and merits?

Why is the Quran in Arabic?

When scholars looked at Arabic sentences, they divided them into two categories. They said, every sentence is either a poem or prose. When the Quran was revealed, the scholars were perplexed. They could not classify these writings as poetry because they were not poems, nor could they classify them as prose because they weren't prose either. So the scholars were forced to add a new category. From this time the scholars of the Arabic language said 'Arabic speech will either be a poem, prose or the Quran'. So the Quran opened a new door for the Arabs, because as it was neither a poem, nor prose, it was its own, third category called 'the Quran'.

The Arabic language has a root system, where words are derived from a root form. Each root form is the base from which you can derive many different words. For example, the base form (دَرَسَ) means 'to study'. If you change it to (يُدَرِّسُ), it means 'to teach', if you change it further to (مَدْرَسة), it means 'a place where you study' i.e. school. The point is that with one basic root, just by making small changes such as adding or deleting a letter, the form and meaning alter. There can be up to forty distinct derivations from one root in Arabic. You won't find this in any other language in the world.

Scholars who Wrote on the Miracles of the Quran

Scholars have written many books on this specific subject of the miracles of the Quran. Some are from the early days and others are from more recent times. Here is a list of some of the authors and the titles of the books they wrote:

Scholars from the early generations	
Author	**Book Title**
زمخشري Zamakhsharee	الكشَّاف Al-Kashaaf
خطابي Khattabee	اعجاز القران I'Jazul Quran
باقلاني Baqillani	اعجاز القران I'Jazul Quran
جرجاني Jurjani	دلائل الاعجاز Dalailul I'Jaz
قرطبي Qurtubi	جامع لاحكام القران Jami Lilhkam Al Quran
آلوسي A'aloosi	روح المعاني Ruhul Ma'ani

More Recent Scholars	
Author	**Book Title**
صادق الرفاعي Sadiq Al Rifai	اعجاز القران والبلاغ النبوية I'Jazul Quran Wal Balag Al Nabwiyyah
عبد الله دراز Abdullah Darraz	النبأ العظيم An Nabaul Azeem
سيد قطب Sayyed Qutub	التصوير الفني في القران Al Tasweer Al Fannee fil Quran

Perfection of every word and letter in the Quran

One of the scholars of the Arabic language by the name of Imam Ismaee رحمة الله عليه would often sit in the court of Haroon Al Rasheed, who was a great ruler of his time. Imam Ismaee رحمة الله عليه was a scholar in the Arabic language and he gave regular lectures in large gatherings. One day, during a lecture he quoted a verse from Chapter 5 of the Quran; Surah Ma'idah, verse 38:

$$وَالسَّارِقُ وَالسَّارِقَةُ فَاقْطَعُوا أَيْدِيَهُمَا جَزَاءً بِمَا كَسَبَا نَكَالًا مِنَ اللهِ وَاللهُ غَفُورٌ رَحِيمٌ$$

As for the thief, male or female, cut off his or her hands: a retribution for their deed and exemplary punishment from Allah and Allah is Forgiving, Most Merciful. (Quran 5:38)

A person stood up from the gathering and said, "O, Ismaee, whose speech is this?" "It's the speech of Allah." The man said, "I swear by Allah, this is not the speech of Allah." Ismaee said, "This is the speech of Allah," and again the man insisted, "This is not the speech of Allah." "Have you memorized the Quran?" He replied, "No." "I am quoting to you a verse from Surah Ma'idah." "No, it is impossible that this verse is from the Quran." Ismaee said, "Let us bring the Quran." The Quran was brought and he opened it at Surah Ma'idah verse 38 and he read:

$$وَالسَّارِقُ وَالسَّارِقَةُ فَاقْطَعُوا أَيْدِيَهُمَا جَزَاءً بِمَا كَسَبَا نَكَالًا مِنَ اللهِ وَاللهُ عَزِيزٌ حَكِيمٌ$$

As for the thief, male or female, cut off his or her hands: a retribution for their deed and exemplary punishment from Allah and Allah is Exalted in Power, full of Wisdom. (Quran 5:38)

Ismaee found his mistake. The ending of the verse is not:

$$وَاللهُ غَفُورٌ رَحِيمٌ$$

Allah is Forgiving, Most Merciful. It is:

$$وَاللهُ عَزِيزٌ حَكِيمٌ$$

Allah is Exalted in Power, full of Wisdom.

People were shocked, they were surprised that this person knew this verse, when he had not memorised the Quran. How was he able to spot the mistake Ismaee had made? So the man explained, "Ismaee! You recited:

$$\text{وَالسَّارِقُ وَالسَّارِقَةُ فَاقْطَعُوا أَيْدِيَهُمَا جَزَاءً بِمَا كَسَبَا نَكَالًا مِنَ اللَّهِ}$$

As for the thief, male or female, cut off his or her hands: a retribution for their deed and exemplary punishment from Allah (Quran 5:38)

This is a case of might and wisdom, this is not a case of forgiveness and mercy. So, if this is not a case of forgiveness and mercy, then how can you say:

$$\text{وَاللَّهُ غَفُورٌ رَحِيمٌ}$$

Allah is Forgiving, Most Merciful.

This story points to the language of the Quran, and the high degree of its eloquence. It illustrates the miracle of the Quran itself, in that every word, letter, and dot is in its correct place. There is not a single word, letter or even a dot that is misplaced.

What is a Miracle?

Before we start to discuss the miracles in the Quran we need to first understand what a miracle is.

A miracle is defined as an effect or extraordinary event in the physical world that surpasses all known human or natural powers and is ascribed to a supernatural cause. (Dictionary.com)

In short, a miracle is an impossibility, something beyond human capacity. Any miracles performed by the Prophets of Allah were performed *by* Allah. The stick of Moses ﷺ turning into a snake, Jesus ﷺ giving life to the dead, with Allah's permission. These acts are beyond human capacity and therefore, we regard them as miracles. There are three conditions that must be met for a true miracle that is from Allah.

1.   The miracle must be from Allah. For example, the miracle of the splitting of the Moon and parting the sea. Allah says:

$$\text{وَمَا كَانَ لِرَسُولٍ أَنْ يَأْتِيَ بِآيَةٍ إِلَّا بِإِذْنِ اللَّهِ}$$

And it was never the part of an apostle to bring a Sign except as Allah permitted (or commanded) (Quran 13:38)

2.   The miracle must verify the claimant's Prophethood rather than the opposite, as in the case of Musaylamah Kazzab, who claimed to be a Prophet of God. When a child was brought to him, he spread his hands on the child and the child died. So this 'miracle' revealed his claim to Prophethood to be false.

3.   The miracle must be unique, in a sense that no other human being is able to accomplish or reproduce the like of it.

The Difference Between the Miracle of the Quran and Other Miracles

When Allah created human beings, in order to guide them on the straight path, He sent Prophets. In order to help the Prophets with their mission, Allah also supported them with miracles. However, there is a fundamental difference between the miracle of the Quran and all other miracles that were given to the Prophets. What is this difference?

1.   The miracle of the Quran is a challenge to every single human being, unlike the other miracles, such as the splitting of the Moon. The Quran came to a people renowned for their exceptional linguistic expertise. They would take pride in their language. So Allah challenged them, "This is your language, Arabic, so try to produce something like the Quran," and they couldn't do it.

2.   All the other Prophets' miracles were something visual. For example, the miracle of Jesus ﷺ bringing the dead back to life, with the permission of Allah, was visual. It was something for the eyes to witness. Likewise, the miracle of Moses ﷺ when Allah parted the sea for him, was something for the eyes to marvel at. Similarly, all the miracles that the Prophets were given, were visual. But the miracle of the Quran is not something to see, it is something for the ears to listen to. That is why in the Quran Allah says:

$$إِنَّا سَمِعْنَا قُرْآنًا عَجَبًا$$

We have really heard a wonderful Recital! (Quran 72:1)

$$سَمِعْنَا وَأَطَعْنَا$$

We hear and we obey. (Quran 24:51)

There are many other verses in the Quran speaking to us about hearing the Quran and listening to it. So the Quran is a miracle of listening, it is a miracle of hearing, an aural miracle and thus, unlike other miracles. All the previous Prophets performed visual miracles, their miracle was not something for the ears to listen to. This differentiates between the miracle of the Quran and other miracles.

3.　All the miracles of the Prophets before Prophet Muhammad ﷺ were time and place-bound. The miracle of Jesus ﷺ bringing the dead to life, with Allah's permission, the miracle of the stick of Moses ﷺ turning into a snake, we believe in them because the Quran tells us their stories. However, if you were to tell someone to believe in the miracle of Jesus ﷺ they could say, 'Well, I didn't see that miracle so how can I believe it? I was not there at the time of Jesus ﷺ.' When you come to the miracle of the Quran, you don't need to be living at the time of Prophet Muhammad ﷺ. The Quran was a miracle yesterday, it is still a miracle today and it will remain a miracle until the Day of Judgement.

That's why the miracle of the Quran is not time-bound, neither it is place-bound; i.e., it does not matter which era you are living in, it does not matter whether you are living at the time of Muhammad ﷺ or living in the 21st century, if you want to experience the miracle of the Quran, you can do that today. It does not matter which location you are in, whether you are in Makkah, the UK or the USA, you can still participate in the miracle of the Quran wherever you are. The Quran came as a miracle for all times.

قُلْ يَا أَيُّهَا النَّاسُ إِنِّي رَسُولُ اللَّهِ إِلَيْكُمْ جَمِيعًا الَّذِي لَهُ مُلْكُ السَّمَاوَاتِ وَالْأَرْضِ ۖ لَا إِلَٰهَ إِلَّا هُوَ يُحْيِي وَيُمِيتُ ۖ فَآمِنُوا بِاللَّهِ وَرَسُولِهِ النَّبِيِّ الْأُمِّيّ

Say: "O men! I am sent unto you all as the apostle of Allah to Whom belongeth the dominion of the Heavens and the Earth: there is no God but He: it is He that giveth both life and death. So believe in Allah and His apostle the unlettered Prophet. (Quran 7:158)

4.　All the Prophets before Prophet Muhammad ﷺ were sent with miracles and with a message. The miracle was to demonstrate and prove their Prophethood and the message was to worship Allah. But when it comes to the miracle of Muhammad ﷺ, his supreme miracle was the Quran and his message was also the Quran. The Quran has two qualities in one. It is a miracle and it is a message at the same time.

Quran - The Greatest Miracle of Muhammad ﷺ

The earlier Prophets got miracles like the parting of the sea for Moses ﷺ, the miracle of bringing the dead to life, with Allah's permission, for Jesus ﷺ. These were indeed great miracles given to these Prophets. Someone may say, 'Well, these are all awesome miracles, how come Prophet Muhammad ﷺ only got a book as his greatest miracle?'

To answer this, suppose you were present at the time of Moses ﷺ and you witnessed his miracle, you would probably believe in it, because you saw the miracle with your own eyes. Then you tell your children, 'I saw the miracle of Moses ﷺ so I believe in his Prophethood.' Your children may believe you because, 'My father saw the miracle.' Then your children tell their children and they tell their children, and so on. Five generations down, when they are told about the miracle of Moses ﷺ, do you think they will have the same level of conviction as you had, when you saw the miracle of Moses ﷺ? Probably not. So, because Muhammad ﷺ is a Prophet for the whole of mankind until the Day of Judgement, his miracle should also be a miracle until the Day of Judgement.

Another reason why the Prophet ﷺ was given a book as his greatest miracle is because if Allah had given the same kind of miracles to Muhammad ﷺ as He did with earlier Prophets, the doubters would have felt justified in their scepticism. In fact, they would say, 'This is magic.' Allah tells us in the Quran about these disbelievers:

وَلَوْ فَتَحْنَا عَلَيْهِمْ بَابًا مِنَ السَّمَاءِ فَظَلُّوا فِيهِ يَعْرُجُونَ (١٤) لَقَالُوا إِنَّمَا سُكِّرَتْ أَبْصَارُنَا بَلْ نَحْنُ قَوْمٌ مَسْحُورُونَ

Even if We opened out to them a gate from Heaven and they were to continue (all day) ascending therein. They would only say: "Our eyes have been intoxicated: nay we have been bewitched by sorcery." (Quran 15:14-15)

There are many stories in which the disbelievers of Makkah demanded miracles from Muhammad ﷺ, and when they saw the miracle they said, 'This is magic.'

A group of people from the Quraish tribe came to the Prophet ﷺ and said: 'O Muhammad, if you are really a Prophet and a messenger then bring to us a miracle.' So he asked them, 'What do you want?' They said, 'Split the Moon for us.' The Prophet ﷺ supplicated to Allah, and Allah ordered him to gesture towards the Moon with his fingers. The Moon split into two parts standing far apart from each other for several hours, then clung back together. Upon seeing this miracle, the pagans started claiming, 'Muhammad ﷺ has practised witchcraft on us!'

One of the leaders of the Quraish tribe named Abdullah Ibn Umayyah Al Makhzoomee said to Muhammad ﷺ, 'O Muhammad, by Allah, I will never believe in you unless you raise a ladder to Heaven and ascend it while I am watching, and then you bring back with you an open book and four angels to testify that you are as you say. By Allah, even if you did that, I think that I would not believe you.' After this incident, Allah revealed the following verses:

وَقَالُوا لَنْ نُؤْمِنَ لَكَ حَتَّىٰ تَفْجُرَ لَنَا مِنَ الْأَرْضِ يَنْبُوعًا (٩٠) أَوْ تَكُونَ لَكَ جَنَّةٌ مِنْ نَخِيلٍ وَعِنَبٍ فَتُفَجِّرَ الْأَنْهَارَ خِلَالَهَا تَفْجِيرًا (٩١) أَوْ تُسْقِطَ السَّمَاءَ كَمَا زَعَمْتَ عَلَيْنَا كِسَفًا أَوْ تَأْتِيَ بِاللَّهِ وَالْمَلَائِكَةِ قَبِيلًا (٩٢) أَوْ يَكُونَ لَكَ بَيْتٌ مِنْ زُخْرُفٍ أَوْ تَرْقَىٰ فِي السَّمَاءِ وَلَنْ نُؤْمِنَ لِرُقِيِّكَ حَتَّىٰ تُنَزِّلَ عَلَيْنَا كِتَابًا نَقْرَؤُهُ ۗ قُلْ سُبْحَانَ رَبِّي هَلْ كُنْتُ إِلَّا بَشَرًا رَسُولًا

They say, "We shall not believe in thee until thou causest a spring to gush forth for us from the Earth, Or (until) thou hast a garden of date trees and vines, and causest rivers to gush forth in their midst, carrying abundant water; Or thou causest the sky to fall in pieces as thou sayest (will happen) against us; or thou bringest Allah and the angels before (us) face to face; Or thou hast a house adorned with gold or thou mountest a ladder right into the skies. No, we shall not even believe in thy mounting until thou sendest down to us a book that we could read." Say: "Glory to my Lord! Am I aught but a man an apostle?" (Quran 17:90-93)

The third reason why Muhammad ﷺ was not given miracles in the same way as the earlier Prophets, was because all the other miracles were small compared to the miracle of the Quran. Every miracle in itself was a great miracle, a great sign from Allah, but compared to the Quran it was small. That is why Allah asks us in the Quran, 'Is the Quran in itself not enough?'

أَوَلَمْ يَكْفِهِمْ أَنَّا أَنْزَلْنَا عَلَيْكَ الْكِتَابَ يُتْلَىٰ عَلَيْهِمْ ۚ إِنَّ فِي ذَٰلِكَ لَرَحْمَةً وَذِكْرَىٰ لِقَوْمٍ يُؤْمِنُونَ

And is it not enough for them that We have sent down to thee the Book which is rehearsed to them? Verily in it is Mercy and a Reminder to those who believe. (Quran 29:51)

The fourth reason was because of Allah's mercy granted to the Quraish, for the disbelievers. It is the custom of Allah that when He sends a miracle after it has been demanded, and then the people don't believe in it, Allah's punishment descends, and He punishes the disbelievers more than He has ever punished anyone else before.

In the story of Jesus ﷺ when his people demanded a miracle, they requested 'a table spread with food, to eat from, so that we know that you are a true messenger from Allah.' So Jesus ﷺ supplicated to Allah to fulfil their demand. Allah replied:

إِنِّي مُنَزِّلُهَا عَلَيْكُمْ ۖ فَمَنْ يَكْفُرْ بَعْدُ مِنْكُمْ فَإِنِّي أُعَذِّبُهُ عَذَابًا لَا أُعَذِّبُهُ أَحَدًا مِنَ الْعَالَمِينَ

I will send it down unto you, but if any of you after that resisteth faith I will punish him with a penalty such as I have not inflicted on anyone among all the peoples. (Quran 5:115)

In the story of Pharaoh, Allah showed them signs after signs. They rejected all the signs and so Allah punished them.

وَلَقَدْ جَاءَ آلَ فِرْعَوْنَ النُّذُرُ (٤١) كَذَّبُوا بِآيَاتِنَا كُلِّهَا فَأَخَذْنَاهُمْ أَخْذَ عَزِيزٍ مُقْتَدِرٍ

To the people of Pharaoh too aforetime came Warners (from Allah). The (people) rejected all Our Signs; but We seized them with such Penalty (as comes) from One Exalted in Power able to carry out His Will. (Quran 54:41-42)

When Allah talks about the she-camel He gave to Salih ﷺ, Allah told the people of Salih ﷺ:

وَلَا تَمَسُّوهَا بِسُوءٍ فَيَأْخُذَكُمْ عَذَابُ يَوْمٍ عَظِيمٍ

"Touch her not with harm lest the penalty of a Great Day seize you." (Quran 26:156)

So this is the custom of Allah, that when He sends a miracle after it has been demanded by the people and then they don't believe in it, Allah's punishment descends. So when Allah does not send the miracle they are demanding, it is a mercy for those disbelievers, because Allah knew that they were not asking for the miracles to believe in Him, they were demanding out of disbelief and stubbornness.

In fact, in a Hadith the Prophet ﷺ was asked by Allah, "If you wish, we will give them what they are asking, but if they then disbelieve, I will punish them with a punishment that I have never imposed upon anyone else in the universe; or, if you wish, I will open for them the gate of repentance and mercy." The Prophet ﷺ said:

بَلْ تَفْتَحُ لَهُم بَابَ التوبَةِ والرَحْمَةِ

"Rather You open for them the gate of repentance and mercy" (Musnad Ahmed 1:242)

That is why when Allah did not give them the signs according to their demands, it was because of the mercy of Allah. If He had given them those signs and they had rejected them, then Allah would have punished them like He had never punished anyone else in the universe.

What did the Quraish find Miraculous about the Quran?

The Quran talks about many subjects and the miracles of the Quran are treated in various areas. There are scientific miracles in the Quran. There are miracles in the legislation and laws that the Quran has laid down for us which are suitable for all times until the Day of Judgement. But these miracles did not amaze the Quraish. What the Quraish found miraculous about the Quran was its language, its style, and its eloquence. There are many stories that illlustrate that what they found miraculous was the Quran's language.

Abu Dharr ؓ says, "I left my home with my brother 'Unais'. During our stay we had a discussion about the Prophet ﷺ." Unais was one of the poets, and he asked Abu Dharr ؓ, "What do the people say about Muhammad ﷺ?" He replied, "They say that he is a poet, or a soothsayer, or a magician." Unais said, "I have heard the words of the soothsayers, and he is not a soothsayer. I compared his words to the words of the poet and no one after me can say that he is a poet. By Allah, he is telling the truth and they are lying." (Muslim)

Umar ؓ, before he accepted Islam, was a strong, hard hearted, and an enemy of Islam and of Muhammad ﷺ. His heart was never softened to Islam, so much so, that one day he decided to kill Muhammad ﷺ. So he took his sword and he set off on his way to kill Muhammad ﷺ. One of the Companions saw him and asked him, "Where are you going?", "To kill Muhammad." The Companion said, "Well, why don't you first look at your own family who have accepted Islam?" Umar ؓ said, "And who is that?", "Your sister Fatimah and her husband Saeed ibn Zayd." Umar ؓ stomped away to his sister's house, banged on the door, and entered the house. He began to hit his sister and her husband. As he was hitting them some pages of the Quran fell out. "Give me those papers!" said Umar ؓ , he began to read the following verses of the Quran:

طه (١) مَا أَنْزَلْنَا عَلَيْكَ الْقُرْآنَ لِتَشْقَىٰ (٢) إِلَّا تَذْكِرَةً لِمَنْ يَخْشَىٰ (٣) تَنْزِيلًا مِمَّنْ خَلَقَ الْأَرْضَ وَالسَّمَاوَاتِ الْعُلَى (٤) الرَّحْمَٰنُ عَلَى الْعَرْشِ اسْتَوَىٰ (٥) لَهُ مَا فِي السَّمَاوَاتِ وَمَا فِي الْأَرْضِ وَمَا بَيْنَهُمَا وَمَا تَحْتَ الثَّرَىٰ

Ta Ha We have not sent down the Quran to thee as a cause of distress to thee. But only as an admonition to those who fear (Allah) – A revelation from Him Who created the Earth and the Heavens on high. (Allah) Most Gracious is firmly established on the Throne (of authority). To Him belongs what is in the Heavens and on Earth, and all between them, and all beneath the soil. (Quran 20:1-6)

When Umar ؓ read these verses he began to shake, and tremble and he said, "These are not the words of a human being." He said, "I bear witness that there is no god but Allah and I bear witness that Muhammad ﷺ is His Messenger.

What was in the Quran that shook Umar ؓ? it was the miracle of its language, its style and its eloquence.

Muhammad ﷺ is not the author of the Quran

The Glorious Quran was revealed upon Muhammed ﷺ but the author of the Quran is none other than Allah. In this section we'll go through several of proofs that proves the Muhammed ﷺ is not the author of the Quran:

1.   The Prophet ﷺ told his companions not to mix the Hadith (sayings of the Prophet) with the Quran. If the Prophet ﷺ had wanted, he could have mixed the Quran and the Hadith together, but he did not.

2.   There are many instances when, if a revelation was revealed at a specific time, it would have benefited the Prophet ﷺ. For example, when his beloved wife Aishah ؓ was slandered, for one month no revelation was revealed, and the Prophet ﷺ suffered anxiety for the whole month. If the Quran had been Muhammad's own composition ﷺ, why would he have had to wait for the revelation? If Muhammad had been the author of the Quran ﷺ, he would immediately have composed new verses for his own benefit and convenience. This never happened, in fact, only after a whole month of prolonged stress and unbearable tensions, Allah revealed in the Quran those verses that exonerated Aishah ؓ from the accusations.

3.   There were many verses in the Quran that were revealed which questioned Muhammad ﷺ: Why did he do this, or why didn't he do this? For example, Allah says:

يَا أَيُّهَا النَّبِيُّ لِمَ تُحَرِّمُ مَا أَحَلَّ اللَّهُ لَكَ

O Prophet! Why holdest thou to be forbidden that which Allah has made lawful to thee? (Quran 66:1)

In another verse of the Quran, Allah tells Muhammad ﷺ not to do certain things. If the Quran was written by Muhammad ﷺ, why would he tell himself not to do certain things? Allah specifically prohibits Muhammad ﷺ from doing certain things. Allah says:

وَلَا تُصَلِّ عَلَىٰ أَحَدٍ مِنْهُمْ مَاتَ أَبَدًا وَلَا تَقُمْ عَلَىٰ قَبْرِهِ

Nor do thou ever pray for any of them that dies nor stand at his grave. (Quran 9:84)

There are many verses that were revealed cautioning Muhammad ﷺ. If the author of the Quran was Muhammed ﷺ then why would he caution himself?

وَلَا تَعْجَلْ بِالْقُرْآنِ مِنْ قَبْلِ أَنْ يُقْضَىٰ إِلَيْكَ وَحْيُهُ

Be not in haste with the Quran before its revelation to thee is completed. (Quran 20:114)

لَا تُحَرِّكْ بِهِ لِسَانَكَ لِتَعْجَلَ بِهِ

Move not thy tongue concerning the (Quran) to make haste therewith. (Quran 75:16)

So all these verses prove that if Muhammed ﷺ was the author of the Quran then he addressing himself in the Quran is meaningless.

4.   There were certain occurrences in the life of Muhammad ﷺ that show he did not know the Unseen. When we look at the story of 'Hudaybiyyah', the Prophet ﷺ had a dream that he entered Makkah and performed tawaaf around the ka'abah. When he told his Companions of this dream, they were happy and they started to prepare for their journey to perform umrah. The Quraish stopped them whilst they were on their way to Makkah and told them to turn back. Umar ؓ came to the Prophet ﷺ and said: "You had a dream that we were doing the umrah, so why can't we do the umrah?" The Prophet ﷺ replied, "Did I say we will do umrah this year? Yes, the dream is true, but I don't know when we will do umrah. We will do umrah, but when we will perform umrah, we don't know." This incident shows that the Prophet ﷺ did not know the Unseen.

5.   Muhammad ﷺ was known as (الصادق الامين - the truthful and the trustworthy) amongst his People.

When the Prophet ﷺ went up to the Heavens in the Night of Ascension, the following morning the Prophet ﷺ told the people about his night journey. One of the disbelievers came to Abu Bakr ؓ and said, "have you heard what your friend is telling the people?; in one night he went up to the Heavens and came back, do you believe that?" Abu Bakr ﷺ replied, "I believe him in signs greater than this. I believe in the revelations that come to him in seconds from the Heavens."

Prophet Muhammed ﷺ was not known as 'the truthful and the trustworthy' only amongst the Muslims, even amongst the disbelievers he was known as the truthful and the trustworthy.

Abu Sufyan, before his acceptance of Islam, was questioned by King Heraclius of Byzantium. He asked Abu Sufyan who was not a Muslim at that time, "Have you ever accused him of telling lies before his claim (to be a Prophet)?" Abu Sufyan said, "No." So, even amongst his enemies he was known as the truthful and the trustworthy.

All these points prove that Muhammad ﷺ was not the author of the Quran; the Quran is a revelation from Allah to Muhammad ﷺ.

Summary

So far, you have had a basic introduction to the miracles of the Quran and the importance of studying these miracles. All Muslims know that the Quran is the miracle of miracles, but many of us do not know what is in the Quran that really makes this book miraculous. Once you study these miracles then the next time you hold the Quran you will realize that you are not holding a mere book in your hands, but that you are holding a miracle.

Workshop

The following test questions and exercises are provided as an additional aid to reinforce your understanding; it is not a necessary requirement to answer all of the questions in the quiz. It is sufficient for the present purposes simply to do one's best to answer as many of the questions as one can. In any case it is advised to go back through the chapter in order to assess your answers.

Quiz 1

1. What is a miracle?
2. What is the difference between the miracle of the Quran and other miracles?

3. Why is the Quran the greatest miracle of Muhammad ﷺ?

4. Give three evidences that Muhammad ﷺ is not the author of the Quran.

5. Identify a story that shows how the power of the Quran affected the disbelievers.

The Effect of the Quran on the Disbelievers and the Challenge of the Quran

DAY 2

The Demand of the Quraish

The Quraish demanded to know why the Quran was revealed to Prophet Muhammad ﷺ. Why couldn't it be revealed to 'one of us'?" By 'one of us' they meant either Waleed Ibn Mughayrah or Urwah Ibn Masood. They said, "If the Quran is revealed to one of these leaders we will accept Islam." Allah revealed the following verse and said:

$$أَهُمْ يَقْسِمُونَ رَحْمَتَ رَبِّكَ$$

Is it they who would portion out the Mercy of thy Lord? (Quran 43:32)

Meaning, they do not choose to whom the Quran is revealed. It is for Allah to decide, and He knows best whom the Quran should be revealed to.

Disbelievers Believed that the Quran was a Revelation from Allah

Once during the Hajj season, Waleed gathered the people of Makkah and said to them, "Let's all agree upon one thing about Muhammad". Some of them said, "He is a (كاهن – soothsayer)", Waleed said, "No, this is not the speech of a soothsayer."

Then they said he is a (مجنون – madman). Waleed said, "No, he is not a madman, he converses with people and there are no signs of insanity, so this is not the speech of a madman." Then they suggested that he is a (شاعر – poet). Waleed said, "No, we know poetry, poetry is our speciality, and this is definitely not poetry." So, they proposed that he is a (ساحر – magician). Waleed refused and said, "No, this is not the speech of a magician either." Then Waleed being a disbeliever made the following statement about the Quran:

والله ما يشبه الذي يقول شيئا من هذا والله إن لقوله الذي يقول حلاوة وإن عليه لطلاوة وإنه لمثمر أعلاه مغدق أسفله وأنه ليعلو ولا يعلى عليه وأنه ليحطم ما تحته

"By God! The words spoken by this person resemble none of these. By God! It is very pleasant and lively. Its branches are laden with fruit. Its roots are well watered. It will definitely dominate and nothing will be able to dominate it, and it will crush everything below it."

Abu Jahl came to Waleed and said to him, "If people hear this statement of yours, they will accept Islam. Don't say such words." So he said, "Let me think this over for a few days." Some days later Abu Jahl asked Waleed, "What are your thoughts about Muhammad and the Quran?" Waleed replied:

سحر يؤثر — وانه سحر يفرق بين المرء وزوجه

"It is magic, the kind of magic that separates husband and wife."

So they all agreed with this evaluation that Muhammad ﷺ was a magician. Allah revealed the following verses in the Quran:

ذَرْنِي وَمَنْ خَلَقْتُ وَحِيدًا

Leave Me Alone (to deal) with the (creature) whom I created (bare and) alone! (Quran 74:11)

سَأُصْلِيهِ سَقَرَ (٢٦) وَمَا أَدْرَاكَ مَا سَقَرُ (٢٧) لَا تُبْقِي وَلَا تَذَرُ

Soon I will cast him into Hell-Fire! And what will explain to thee what Hell-Fire is? Naught doth it permit to endure and naught doth it leave alone! (Quran 74:26-28)

The Quran overwhelmed the Quraish leaders. They were so obsessed with the Quran that they could not stop themselves from listening to it. They would stop others from listening to it, but they themselves could not resist the urge to listen to the Quran.

One night, three Quraish leaders by the names of Abu Sufyan, Akhnas ibn Shurayh and Abu Jahl left their homes. The Prophet ﷺ would wake up in the last part of the night for his night prayers and would recite the Quran in his salah. So, one night, each of the three leaders came out, secretly, each hoping not to be seen by anyone, because if their own people were to have caught them in the act, it would have meant trouble. So, they sat listening to the Quran while the Prophet ﷺ recited it in his Salah. As they were listening, they were overwhelmed by the recitation. When the recitation ended and they each set off, the three leaders were shocked to see each other so unexpectedly as they made their separate ways home. They admitted to each other that their reason for coming out at night was to listen to the recitation of the Quran. Each promised the others that they would not come again. However, the next night, all three of them came out again to listen to the Quran, once more they promised each other that they would not do so again. On the third night they unexpectedly met each other again and once more they promised they would never repeat it. They had become obsessed with the Quran. They were Non-Muslims, they were disbelievers, but they could not stop themselves from listening to the Quran.

Acceptance of Islam upon Hearing the Quran

The Quraish leaders decided to warn people not to listen to Muhammad ﷺ. They also decided to warn not only the people of Makkah but also the leaders of other tribes who would come to Makkah for the Hajj. During one Hajj season, one of the leaders of the *Daws* tribe arrived in Makkah. His name was Tufayl Ibn Amar Al Dawsee. The leaders of the Quraish approached him to warn him against Muhammad ﷺ. They said to him, "Do not listen to Muhammad, he has separated men from women, he has separated the tribes and people with his magic. So stay away from him and do not listen to him." As Tufayl Ibn Amar Al Dawsee began to perform tawaaf around the ka'abah, he put wool in his ears so that he could not hear the Quran. Tufayl was a poet, and as he was performing his tawaaf he said to himself, "I am a poet, and I will not be affected by the recitation of the Quran." So he took the wool out of his ears, and sat next to Muhammad ﷺ. When Tufayl heard the Quran, he immediately accepted Islam.

Why did this leader of the *Daws* tribe accept Islam? It was not because of the laws and legislation, as the laws were not revealed in Makkah, they were revealed in Madinah. He accepted Islam because of the beauty of the Quran, its style and its eloquence.

The Effect of the Quran on Utbah Ibn Rabeeah

Utbah Ibn Rabeeah, one of the leaders of the Quraish, decided one day that they should all together make an agreement with Muhammad ﷺ. So they went to Muhammad ﷺ and Utbah Ibn Rabeeah said, "O' Muhammed, Whatever you want from us we will give you. You want wealth? We will give you wealth, you want status? We will give you status, you want power? We will give you power, you want women? We will give you women. Whatever you want we will give you, but stop spreading the message of the Quran." Muhammad ﷺ asked him, "Have you finished, O' Utbah?" "yes." The Prophet ﷺ said, listen to this, and he recited:

حم (١) تَنْزِيلٌ مِنَ الرَّحْمَنِ الرَّحِيمِ (٢) كِتَابٌ فُصِّلَتْ آيَاتُهُ قُرْآنًا عَرَبِيًّا لِقَوْمٍ يَعْلَمُونَ (٣) بَشِيرًا وَنَذِيرًا فَأَعْرَضَ أَكْثَرُهُمْ فَهُمْ لَا يَسْمَعُونَ

Ha Mim. A Revelation from (Allah) Most Gracious, Most Merciful— A Book, whereof the verses are explained in detail— a Quran in Arabic, for people who understand— Giving Good News and Admonition: yet most of them turn away, and so they hear not. (Quran 41:1-4)

He continued to recite until Allah's statement:

فَإِنْ أَعْرَضُوا فَقُلْ أَنْذَرْتُكُمْ صَاعِقَةً مِثْلَ صَاعِقَةِ عَادٍ وَثَمُودَ

But if they turn away, say thou: "I have warned you of a stunning Punishment (as of thunder and lightning) like that which (overtook) the 'Ad and the Thamud!" (Quran 41:13)

When the Prophet ﷺ reached this verse, Utbah Ibn Rabeeah was terrified and he began to shake. He placed his hands over the mouth of the Prophet ﷺ and said, "Stop! Do not recite any more!" The Prophet ﷺ continued reciting until he reached the verse of prostration, he prostrated before Allah and glorified Him in his prostration.

Utbah was speechless, he couldn't say anything. He stood up and went back to his people. People said that Utbah's face had changed. He had left with one face and had come back with a different face. They asked him, "What happened?" He replied, "Leave Muhammad alone." They said, "We can't leave him." He said, "This is not poetry, neither is it magic, this is something different." The Quraish said, "We cannot just leave him," so they insisted, "This is magic." ·

The Challenge of Allah

Allah revealed the 'Muqatta'at' letters, i.e the unique letter combinations (الم — حم — كهيعص). These letters were revealed to challenge the disbelievers: "These are your letters, you make poems with these letters, so with these letters try to use them to create a Quran like this."

قُلْ لَئِنِ اجْتَمَعَتِ الْإِنْسُ وَالْجِنُّ عَلَىٰ أَنْ يَأْتُوا بِمِثْلِ هَٰذَا الْقُرْآنِ لَا يَأْتُونَ بِمِثْلِهِ وَلَوْ كَانَ بَعْضُهُمْ لِبَعْضٍ ظَهِيرًا

Say: "If the whole of mankind and Jinns were to gather together to produce the like of this Quran, they could not produce the like thereof, even if they backed each other up with help and support. (Quran 17:88)

By this Allah is affirming they will never be able to produce anything like the Quran. This challenge is for the past, present and the future. They were not able to produce anything like the Quran then, no one can produce anything like the Quran today, and no one will ever be able to produce anything like the Quran at any time from now until the Day of Judgement.

Their Claim that the Quran is a Storybook

When the disbelievers were challenged to produce a book like the Quran, they said, "This book talks about previous nations, so it's more like a story book." They brought a person by the name of Nadr Ibn Harith from Taif (a city in Arabia), who was an expert storyteller. They said to him, "When Muhammad speaks the Quran, you must start telling us stories." So it transpired.

Allah revealed the following verse in the Quran:

وَقَالُوا أَسَاطِيرُ الْأَوَّلِينَ اكْتَتَبَهَا فَهِيَ تُمْلَىٰ عَلَيْهِ بُكْرَةً وَأَصِيلًا

And they say: "Tales of the ancients which he has caused to be written and they are dictated before him morning and evening." (Quran 25:5)

The stories that Nadr ibn Harith was narrating were stories of the past. Eventually you would become bored with these stories if you were to listen to them day and night. The Quran is not a storybook. It is a book containing laws, guidance, stories, admonitions, warnings, and teachings. All of these are in one book, the Quran. You will get bored listening to stories, but the more you read the Quran, the more fascinating and absorbing it becomes.

Their Claim that the Quran was Produced by a Foreigner

The Quraish said, "This is not a book of Allah, neither are these the words of Muhammad. These are the words of a person who lives in a city called Yamamah who is not an Arab, he is a foreigner." Allah replies to this in the Quran:

$$\text{وَلَقَدْ نَعْلَمُ أَنَّهُمْ يَقُولُونَ إِنَّمَا يُعَلِّمُهُ بَشَرٌ ۗ لِسَانُ الَّذِي يُلْحِدُونَ إِلَيْهِ أَعْجَمِيٌّ وَهَٰذَا لِسَانٌ}$$

$$\text{عَرَبِيٌّ مُبِينٌ}$$

We know indeed that they say "It is a man that teaches him." The tongue of him they wickedly point to is notably foreign, while this is Arabic pure and clear. (Quran 16:103)

The Arabic language of the Quran has reached its height and its peak in eloquence and style. The experts in the Arabic language were left speechless at its beauty. How can you attribute this glorious literary expression to a foreigner who has limited knowledge of the Arabic language?

Allah Makes the Challenge Easy

First the Quraish were challenged to create or discover something similar to the Quran. They could not, saying, "It is too difficult, the Quran talks about the past, stories and history which we don't know, so we cannot meet this challenge." The challenge was then made easier. This time the challenge was to create ten surahs (chapters) of the same quality as the Quran. Any ten surahs, long or short.

$$\text{أَمْ يَقُولُونَ افْتَرَاهُ قُلْ فَأْتُوا بِعَشْرِ سُوَرٍ مِثْلِهِ مُفْتَرَيَاتٍ وَادْعُوا مَنِ اسْتَطَعْتُمْ مِنْ دُونِ اللَّهِ إِنْ}$$

$$\text{كُنْتُمْ صَادِقِينَ}$$

Or they may say, "He forged it." Say: "Bring ye then ten Surahs forged like unto it and call (to your aid) whomsoever ye can other than Allah!— if ye speak the truth!" (Quran 11:13)

When they were unable to bring ten surahs, the challenge became even easier. Allah then challenged them to bring one surah:

$$\text{أَمْ يَقُولُونَ افْتَرَاهُ قُلْ فَأْتُوا بِسُورَةٍ مِثْلِهِ وَادْعُوا مَنِ اسْتَطَعْتُمْ مِنْ دُونِ اللَّهِ إِنْ كُنْتُمْ صَادِقِينَ}$$

Or do they say, "He forged it"? Say: "Bring then a Surah like unto it and call (to your aid) anyone you can besides Allah if it be ye speak the truth!" (Quran 10:38)

The smallest surah consists of just three verses. They couldn't meet this simple challenge. These challenges were not only for the people of Makkah, but also for the people of Madinah. It was also for the Jews, who had knowledge of previous revelations and stories. Everyone was challenged.

The last challenge was revealed in Madinah where Allah asked the people to bring a surah 'somewhat similar':

وَإِنْ كُنْتُمْ فِي رَيْبٍ مِمَّا نَزَّلْنَا عَلَى عَبْدِنَا فَأْتُوا بِسُورَةٍ مِنْ مِثْلِهِ وَادْعُوا شُهَدَاءَكُمْ مِنْ دُونِ اللَّهِ إِنْ كُنْتُمْ صَادِقِينَ (٢٣) فَإِنْ لَمْ تَفْعَلُوا وَلَنْ تَفْعَلُوا فَاتَّقُوا النَّارَ الَّتِي وَقُودُهَا النَّاسُ وَالْحِجَارَةُ أُعِدَّتْ لِلْكَافِرِينَ

And if ye are in doubt as to what We have revealed from time to time to Our servant then produce a Surah like thereunto; and call your witnesses or helpers (if there are any) besides Allah if your (doubts) are true. But if ye cannot and of a surety ye cannot then fear the fire whose fuel is Men and Stones which is prepared for those who reject Faith. (Quran 2: 23-24)

The people could not meet the challenge in Makkah, nor the one in Madinah, and no-one will ever be able to meet them in the time remaining between now and the Day of Judgement.

For those who say, "I do not know Arabic as a language, so how can I produce a Surah like the Quran?" There is a challenge even for them. Allah says:

أَفَلَا يَتَدَبَّرُونَ الْقُرْءَانَ وَلَوْ كَانَ مِنْ عِندِ غَيْرِ اللَّهِ لَوَجَدُوا فِيهِ اخْتِلَافًا كَثِيرًا

Do they not ponder on the Quran (with care)? Had it been from other than Allah, they would surely have found therein much discrepancy. (Quran 4:82)

If you think that this Quran is not from Allah then find one single mistake in it. No one has been able to find a single mistake in the Quran because the author of the Quran is none other than our Creator, Allah.

If you were to tell a story to someone, and tell that same story more than once, the second time there could be some discrepancies between the two narratives. The likelihood of this increases the more times your story is repeated.

In the Quran, Moses's story ﷺ is mentioned in over seventy different places; each story uses different vocabulary and a different style, and no story is at odds with any other.

I challenge anyone to tell the same story ten times, using different vocabulary, without producing contradictions or inconsistencies. We cannot do it, but Allah, the One Who revealed the Quran, is able to do so. That is why, in the Quran, Allah issues a general challenge to produce a book with such style, eloquence and beauty, and the challenge has never been met.

قُلْ لَئِنِ اجْتَمَعَتِ الْإِنْسُ وَالْجِنُّ عَلَىٰ أَنْ يَأْتُوا بِمِثْلِ هٰذَا الْقُرْآنِ لَا يَأْتُونَ بِمِثْلِهِ وَلَوْ كَانَ بَعْضُهُمْ لِبَعْضٍ ظَهِيرًا

Say: "If the whole of mankind and Jinns were to gather together to produce the like of this Quran they could not produce the like thereof, even if they backed up each other with help and support. (Quran 17:88)

People Tried to Produce the Like of the Quran

There were some people who tried to answer the challenge. Musaylamah Kazzab produced some verses:

الْفِيلُ الْفِيلُ وَمَا أَدْرَاكَ مَا الْفِيلُ، لَهُ ذَنَبٌ وَبِيلٌ، وَخُرْطُومٌ طَوِيلٌ

The elephant. The elephant. What is the elephant? And who shall tell you what the elephant is? He has a ropy tail and a long trunk.

And he said:

وَالطَّاحِنَاتُ طَحْنًا، فَالْعَاجِنَاتُ عَجْنًا، فَالْخَابِزَاتُ خَبْزًا، إِهَالَةً وَسَمْنًا، إِنَّ الْأَرْضَ بَيْنَنَا وَبَيْنَ قُرَيْشٍ نِصْفَيْنِ، وَلَكِنَّ قُرَيْشًا قَوْمٌ لَا يَعْدِلُونَ

And he said:

إِنَّا أَعْطَيْنَاكَ الْجَمَاهِرَ، فَصَلِّ لِرَبِّكَ وَهَاجِرْ، وَلَاتُطِعْ كُلَّ سَاحِرٍ وَكَافِرْ

When you listen to these verses, and you then listen to the verses of the Quran, there is a world of difference. When anyone tried to imitate the writing in the Quran, even their own people, their own followers, mocked their writing. Their verses didn't have the message, the guidance, the style, or the eloquence the Quran has. These people they failed to:

1. Replicate the Quran's literary form

2. Match the unique linguistic nature of the Quran

3. Select and arrange words like that of the Quran

4. Select and arrange similar grammatical particles

5. Match the Qurans superior eloquence and sound

6. Equal the frequency of rhetorical devices

7. Match the level of content and informativeness

8. Equal the Quran's conciseness and flexibility

The Quran is not just words that we recite, there is guidance, and there is admonition, all in a very unique style. That's why even their own people, their own followers, mocked the writers when they produced these verses, trying to imitate the Quran.

Miracles of the Unseen in the Quran

There are many things in the Quran that are from the unseen and only Allah knows of. We don't know the future, but Allah knows the future, and so the Quran talks about the future; thus: Miracles of the Unseen.

Islam will Prevail over all other Religions

Allah gives a promise in the Quran that Islam will prevail over all other religions: Christianity, Judaism, Hinduism, Communism and so on. This is what we see today. Islam is the fastest growing religion in the world. This is true in the USA, in the UK, and the fastest growing religion *in the world* is Islam. Allah says:

هُوَ الَّذِي أَرْسَلَ رَسُولَهُ بِالْهُدَىٰ وَدِينِ الْحَقِّ لِيُظْهِرَهُ عَلَى الدِّينِ كُلِّهِ وَلَوْ كَرِهَ الْمُشْرِكُونَ

It is He Who has sent His Messenger with Guidance and the Religion of Truth, that he may proclaim it over all religion, even though the pagans may detest (it). (Quran 61:9)

Muslims will be Victorious

When the Muslims were defeated in the battle of Uhud by one of the tribes of the Jews, the victors were happy and said that Muhammad was not a Prophet. Had he been a Prophet of Allah, the Muslims would not have been defeated. So Allah revealed the following verse, telling the Jews that soon they will be the losers.

قُلْ لِّلَّذِينَ كَفَرُوا سَتُغْلَبُونَ وَتُحْشَرُونَ إِلَىٰ جَهَنَّمَ ۚ وَبِئْسَ الْمِهَادُ

> Say to those who reject Faith: "Soon will ye be vanquished and gathered together to Hell – an evil bed indeed (to lie on)! (Quran 3:12)

This verse of the Quran predicted that the Jews would be defeated. After a short time, Muslims succeeded in defeating two Jewish tribes. The first was Bani Quraydah and the second was Bani An-Nadir in Madinah. Also, after the conquest of Makkah the pagans vanished. How did Muhammad ﷺ know that there would be victory for the Muslims? Because Allah had informed him of it ﷺ.

Romans will be Victorious

الٓمٓ (١) غُلِبَتِ ٱلرُّومُ (٢) فِىٓ أَدْنَى ٱلْأَرْضِ وَهُم مِّنۢ بَعْدِ غَلَبِهِمْ سَيَغْلِبُونَ (٣) فِى بِضْعِ سِنِينَ

> Alif Lam Mim. The Roman Empire has been defeated In a land close by; but they, (even) after (this) defeat of theirs, will soon be victorious Within a few years. (Quran 30:1-4)

This verse tells us that the Romans will be victorious over the Persians and during Muhammad's life ﷺ, the Persians tried to defeat the Romans, so this verse revealed that the Romans would be defeated, and they were. This was the reality at that time. But the Quran gives us a prediction, that the Romans will soon be victorious after their defeat. People were incredulous the disbelievers were shocked, wanting to know how this was possible. The verse further says 'in a few years' and the word (بِضْع) is between 3-9 years. So Allah is saying that in the coming 3-9 years the Romans will be victorious. People were surprised because the Persians were the most powerful people on Earth and were considered invincible However, the Romans defeated the Persians and this is amongst the miracles of the Unseen.

Waleed Ibn Mughairah will not Accept Islam

Allah knew that Waleed would not accept Islam, which is why Allah revealed this verse in the Quran:

سَأُصْلِيهِ سَقَرَ (٢٦) وَمَا أَدْرَاكَ مَا سَقَرُ (٢٧) لَا تُبْقِي وَلَا تَذَرُ

Soon We will cast him into Hell-Fire! And what will explain to thee what Hell-Fire is? Naught doth it permit to endure and naught doth it leave alone! – (Quran 74:26-28)

These verses of the Quran were revealed when Waleed was alive. Allah is telling the Prophet Muhammad ﷺ that Waleed will not accept Islam. As an enemy of Islam, the only thing that Waleed had to do was to say 'I am a Muslim' and the Quran would have been proved wrong. But he did not believe, and Allah knew that he would not accept Islam.

Abu Lahab will not Accept Islam

Allah also knew that Abu Lahab would not accept Islam, and that is why in surah Masad Allah talks about the destruction of Abu Lahab and his wife. Allah says:

سَيَصْلَىٰ نَارًا ذَاتَ لَهَبٍ (٣) وَامْرَأَتُهُ حَمَّالَةَ الْحَطَبِ (٤) فِي جِيدِهَا حَبْلٌ مِنْ مَسَدٍ

Burnt soon will he be in a Fire of blazing Flame! His wife shall carry the (crackling) wood – as fuel! – A twisted rope of palm-leaf fibre around her (own) neck! (Quran 111:3-5)

Both of these people, 'Abu Lahab' and his wife, were alive when this surah was revealed. Allah knew that they would not accept Islam. They were enemies of Islam, and all they had to do to prove the Quran wrong was to say, 'We are Muslims'. They never did, and Allah knew that they would not accept Islam.

Allah knows the future. Allah knew that Abu Lahab, his wife, Abu Jahal and Waleed Ibn Mugairah wouldn't accept Islam.

The Miracle of the Quran's Style and Rhyming

When it comes to the style and the rhythm of the Quran, the Quran has reached the height of Arabic in it, to the extent that no one is able to produce writings in the style of the Quran, or in the way the Quran rhymes. When you look at verses in the Quran, there are changes in style. For example Allah says in the Quran regarding 'Waleed Ibn Mugairah':

ذَرْنِي وَمَنْ خَلَقْتُ وَحِيدًا (١١) وَجَعَلْتُ لَهُ مَالًا مَّمْدُودًا (١٢) وَبَنِينَ شُهُودًا (١٣) وَمَهَّدْتُ لَهُ تَمْهِيدًا (١٤) ثُمَّ يَطْمَعُ أَنْ أَزِيدَ

Leave Me alone (to deal) with the (creature) whom I created (bare and) alone!— To whom I granted resources in abundance, and sons to be by his side!— For whom I made (life) smooth and comfortable! Yet he is greedy— that I should add (yet more) (Quran 74: 11-15)

Read the above verses again, pause at the end of each verse and ponder over the style and the way it rhymes. The first four verses rhyme with the same style, but in the fifth verse both rhyme and rhythm have changed. Why did Allah make these changes in the fifth verse? It has changed to show you that the subject has changed. So with the change of subject, there is a change in the metrical dynamic. A change in rhyme and metre alerts the reciter of a change of subject. These words of the Quran read as though they rhyme, but it is not a poem with the same structure throughout. Though it may rhyme, the style is totally unique.

Sometimes we see that there are verses in the Quran that rhyme, but then the pattern stops. The Quran is not a book of poems. Let us look at these verses and see how the rhyme and rhythm break.

يَٰأُخْتَ هَٰرُونَ مَا كَانَ أَبُوكِ ٱمْرَأَ سَوْءٍ وَمَا كَانَتْ أُمُّكِ بَغِيًّا (٢٨)

فَأَشَارَتْ إِلَيْهِ قَالُوا كَيْفَ نُكَلِّمُ مَن كَانَ فِى ٱلْمَهْدِ صَبِيًّا (٢٩)

قَالَ إِنِّي عَبْدُ ٱللَّهِ ءَاتَٰنِىَ ٱلْكِتَٰبَ وَجَعَلَنِي نَبِيًّا (٣٠)

وَجَعَلَنِي مُبَارَكًا أَيْنَ مَا كُنتُ وَأَوْصَٰنِي بِٱلصَّلَوٰةِ وَٱلزَّكَوٰةِ مَا دُمْتُ حَيًّا (٣١)

وَبَرًّا بِوَٰلِدَتِى وَلَمْ يَجْعَلْنِي جَبَّارًا شَقِيًّا (٣٢)

وَٱلسَّلَٰمُ عَلَىَّ يَوْمَ وُلِدتُّ وَيَوْمَ أَمُوتُ وَيَوْمَ أُبْعَثُ حَيًّا (٣٣)

ذَٰلِكَ عِيسَى ٱبْنُ مَرْيَمَ قَوْلَ ٱلْحَقِّ ٱلَّذِى فِيهِ يَمْتَرُونَ (٣٤)

مَا كَانَ لِلَّهِ أَن يَتَّخِذَ مِن وَلَدٍ سُبْحَنَهُ إِذَا قَضَىٰ أَمْرًا فَإِنَّمَا يَقُولُ لَهُ كُن فَيَكُونُ (٣٥)

"O sister of Aaron! thy father was not a man of evil, nor thy mother a woman unchaste!"

But she pointed to the babe. They said: "How can we talk to one who is a child in the cradle?"

He said: "I am indeed a servant of Allah: He hath given me revelation and made me a Prophet;

"And He hath made me Blessed wheresoever I be, and hath enjoined on me Prayer and Charity as long as I live;

"(He) hath made me kind to my mother, and not overbearing or miserable;

"So Peace is on me the day I was born, the day that I die and the day that I shall be raised up to life (again)"!

Such (was) Jesus the son of Mary: (it is) a statement of truth, about which they (vainly) dispute.

It is not befitting to (the majesty of) Allah that He should beget a son. Glory be to Him! When He determines a matter, He only says to it "Be", and it is. (Quran 19: 28-35)

If you look at the above verses, all the verses rhyme. As you come down and see the last two verses, the rhyming has changed. The reason why it has changed is because the story of Maryam has changed. Once the story is finished, Allah is telling us now what He expects from us, that is why the rhyming has stopped. The proof for this is in the verses that follow, let us continue.

وَإِنَّ ٱللَّهَ رَبِّي وَرَبُّكُمْ فَٱعْبُدُوهُ هَٰذَا صِرَٰطٌ مُّسْتَقِيمٌ (٣٦)

فَٱخْتَلَفَ ٱلْأَحْزَابُ مِنۢ بَيْنِهِمْ فَوَيْلٌ لِّلَّذِينَ كَفَرُوا۟ مِن مَّشْهَدِ يَوْمٍ عَظِيمٍ (٣٧)

أَسْمِعْ بِهِمْ وَأَبْصِرْ يَوْمَ يَأْتُونَنَا لَٰكِنِ ٱلظَّٰلِمُونَ ٱلْيَوْمَ فِى ضَلَٰلٍ مُّبِينٍ (٣٨)

وَأَنذِرْهُمْ يَوْمَ ٱلْحَسْرَةِ إِذْ قُضِىَ ٱلْأَمْرُ وَهُمْ فِى غَفْلَةٍ وَهُمْ لَا يُؤْمِنُونَ (٣٩)

إِنَّا نَحْنُ نَرِثُ ٱلْأَرْضَ وَمَنْ عَلَيْهَا وَإِلَيْنَا يُرْجَعُونَ (٤٠)

Verily Allah is my Lord and your Lord: Him therefore serve ye: this is a Way that is straight.

But the sects differ among themselves: and woe to the Unbelievers because of the (coming) Judgment of a momentous Day!

How plainly will they see and hear, the Day that they will appear before Us! but the unjust today are in error manifest!

But warn them of the Day of Distress, when the matter will be determined: for (behold) they are negligent and they do not believe!

It is We Who will inherit the Earth, and all beings thereon: to Us will they all be returned. (Quran 19: 36-40)

Allah now resumes with the previous rhyming from here. The following verses are:

وَٱذۡكُرۡ فِى ٱلۡكِتَٰبِ إِبۡرَٰهِيمَ إِنَّهُۥ كَانَ صِدِّيقًا نَّبِيًّا (٤١)

إِذۡ قَالَ لِأَبِيهِ يَٰٓأَبَتِ لِمَ تَعۡبُدُ مَا لَا يَسۡمَعُ وَلَا يُبۡصِرُ وَلَا يُغۡنِى عَنكَ شَيۡئًا (٤٢)

يَٰٓأَبَتِ إِنِّى قَدۡ جَآءَنِى مِنَ ٱلۡعِلۡمِ مَا لَمۡ يَأۡتِكَ فَٱتَّبِعۡنِىٓ أَهۡدِكَ صِرَٰطًا سَوِيًّا (٤٣)

Also mention in the Book (the story of) Abraham: he was a man of Truth, a Prophet.

Behold, he said to his father: "O my father! why worship that which heareth not and seeth not, and can profit thee nothing?

"O my father! To me hath come knowledge which hath not reached thee: so follow me: I will guide thee to a Way that is even and straight. (Quran 19: 41-43)

Look at the rhyming of these verses. When Allah finished telling us what He expects from us after narrating the story of Maryam 🕌, He then continues with the same rhyming as He was using in the story of Maryam 🕌. Allah went back to the same rhyming of words. So with the change of subject, there is a change of rhythm. That is why when Allah finishes telling us what He expects from us, He reverts to the rhythm. Glory be to Allah, Who put every letter in its place. Next time when you read the Quran and you notice that the rhythm has changed, it is due to a change of subject.

Changes in the length of Sentences and Rhyming

Like these you will find many examples. For example, in one place of the Quran Allah says:

وَٱلنَّـٰزِعَـٰتِ غَرْقًا (١) وَٱلنَّـٰشِطَـٰتِ نَشْطًا (٢) وَٱلسَّـٰبِحَـٰتِ سَبْحًا (٣) فَٱلسَّـٰبِقَـٰتِ سَبْقًا (٤) فَٱلْمُدَبِّرَٰتِ أَمْرًا (٥) يَوْمَ تَرْجُفُ ٱلرَّاجِفَةُ (٦) تَتْبَعُهَا ٱلرَّادِفَةُ (٧) قُلُوبٌ يَوْمَئِذٍ وَاجِفَةٌ (٨) أَبْصَـٰرُهَا خَـٰشِعَةٌ (٩) يَقُولُونَ أَءِنَّا لَمَرْدُودُونَ فِى ٱلْحَافِرَةِ (١٠) أَءِذَا كُنَّا عِظَـٰمًا نَّخِرَةً (١١) قَالُواْ تِلْكَ إِذًا كَرَّةٌ خَاسِرَةٌ (١٢) فَإِنَّمَا هِىَ زَجْرَةٌ وَٰحِدَةٌ (١٣) فَإِذَا هُم بِٱلسَّاهِرَةِ (١٤) هَلْ أَتَىٰكَ حَدِيثُ مُوسَىٰ (١٥) إِذْ نَادَىٰهُ رَبُّهُۥ بِٱلْوَادِ ٱلْمُقَدَّسِ طُوًى

By the (angels) who tear out (the souls of the wicked) with violence;

By those who gently draw out (the souls of the blessed);

And by those who glide along (on errands of mercy),

Then press forward as in a race,

Then arrange to do (the commands of their Lord)—

One Day everything that can be in commotion will be in violent commotion

Followed by oft-repeated (commotions):

Hearts that Day will be in agitation;

Cast down will be (their owners') eyes.

They say (now): "What! shall we indeed be returned to (our) former state?"

"What!— When we shall have become rotten bones?"

They say: "It would, in that case be a return with loss!"

But verily, it will be but a single (compelling) Cry.

When behold they will be in the (full) awakening (to Judgment).

Has the story of Moses reached thee?

Behold, thy Lord did call to him in the sacred valley to Tuwa

In the last two verses you notice the rhyming has changed. Not only has the rhyming changed, the sentences have increased in length. Why? For the same reason as in the previous example. Due to the change of subject, the rhyming has changed. In the earlier verses Allah was talking about the Day of Judgement, then Allah changed the subject in the last two verses and started to narrate the story of Moses ﷺ and changed the rhyming. Not only that but, when Allah was talking about the Day of Judgement the sentences were short, when Allah was narrating to us the story of Moses ﷺ the sentences became longer. Who could do this? Is this the speech of a human? Glory be to Allah!

Summary

Today, you have learnt how the Quran affected the disbelievers: What they found amazing about the Quran, the reason why they accepted the Quran as a revelation from Allah. The Arabs were so proud of their language that they would boast about it. However, when the Quran was recited to them they had to agree that this book was unique. Its language, style and eloquence were exceptional and that it had to be a revelation from Allah.

You will also have learnt about the challenges of the Quran. The Quran first challenges to attempt to write a book like the Quran. Then the challenges are made progressively easier until Allah challenges to produce a chapter similar to any chapter of the Quran. There were those who tried to produce chapters like the Quran, but when the writings were compared, their language fell short in eloquence, beauty and guidance. The Quran is a unique book, and with all this beauty and style it guides and admonishes us.

Workshop

The quiz questions and the exercises are provided to further your understanding. Don't worry if you can't answer all of the questions in the quiz. Try your best to answer as many as you can. You should go back through the chapter to check your answers.

Quiz 2

1. What was the demand of the Quraish regarding the revelation of the Quran?
2. Recall a story that shows that even the disbelievers believed that this book is a revelation from Allah.
3. Recall a story that shows that the disbelievers were obsessed with the Quran.
4. How did Tufayl Ibn Amar Al Dawsee accept Islam?
5. What is the challenge of the Quran for those who do not know Arabic?
6. Give two examples of the miracles of the unseen in the Quran?
7. Why does the Quran change its style and rhythm?
8. What is the answer to those who tried to produce writings like the Quran?

2

Miracle of the eloquence of the Quran

DAY 3

Which Part of the Quran is a Miracle?

Bandar Alfarisi, a scholar in the Arabic language, was once asked, "Which part of the Quran is a miracle?" He replied, "This question in itself is illogical. It is as though you ask me, 'Which part of the human body is human'? Well, the whole human body is human. Similarly, the whole of the Quran is a miracle. It is not that some parts of it are miraculous whilst the others are not; no, the whole Quran, each and every verse in itself is a miracle."

In today's lesson, I want to share with you some miracles related to the eloquence of the Quran, and by reflecting upon just some of these examples, could change the way you read the Quran forever.

Miracle in a Letter

The example I want to share with you here is of two similar verses where a reader when reading them may not notice the difference between them. Let us compare these verses which illustrates how every letter has been very precisely placed. Allah says:

وَلَمَنْ صَبَرَ وَغَفَرَ إِنَّ ذَٰلِكَ لَمِنْ عَزْمِ الْأُمُورِ

But indeed if any show patience and forgive, that Verily is of the firmness of affairs. (Quran 42:43)

When you read Surah Luqman, Allah mentions a similar verse with just a slight change in it. Allah says:

وَاصْبِرْ عَلَىٰ مَا أَصَابَكَ إِنَّ ذَٰلِكَ مِنْ عَزْمِ الْأُمُورِ

And be patient on whatsoever may befall you; verily that is of the firmness of affairs. (Quran 31:17)

The difference that I want to point out is the ending of both verses. In the first verse Allah says (لَمِنْ عَزْمِ الْأُمُورِ) in the second verse Allah says (مِنْ عَزْمِ الْأُمُورِ). Why does Allah drop the letter (ل) in the second verse?

There are two types of patience. Sometimes patience is required when there is no opponent, and sometimes patience is required and there is an opponent. In the first type of patience, when there is no opponent, and patience is required, then the only thing that it required from this person is patience. For example, a calamity falls upon a person, there is no opponent involved, so the waiting kind of patience is required from a believer. However, in the second type of patience when there is an opponent, then besides patience, there is forgiveness, controlling your tongue, and so forth that is required. This type of patience Allah mentions in Surah Luqman, to emphasize that in this circumstance patience and forgiveness are required.

Therefore Allah uses the letter (ل) and says:

$$لَمِنْ عَزْمِ الْأُمُورِ$$

that Verily is of the firmness of affairs. (Quran 42:43)

This is the type of patience needed when there is an opponent because you have the power to take revenge, it is required of you to be patient and forgive. So this command emphasises patience with forgiveness.

This is just one example of a miracle in one letter. We will look at examples of the miracles in a word, then in a sentence, then in its style and eloquence and so on. This book is not intended as a comprehensive collection of the miracles in every single verse of the Quran; therefore only a limited number of examples will be given just to open the doors for you in this area.

Perfect Choice of Words

In the Arabic language there can be two words which are very similar in meaning, Allah uses one of them instead of the other. We will give you some examples of such verses in the Quran.

Allah says that on the Day of Judgement the Messenger of Allah ﷺ will come to Allah and say:

$$يَا رَبِّ إِنَّ قَوْمِي اتَّخَذُوا هَٰذَا الْقُرْآنَ مَهْجُورًا$$

"O, my Lord! truly my people took this Quran for just foolish nonsense." (Quran 25:30)

The word that Allah uses here is (مَهْجُورًا) which means 'they left the Quran far behind'. Another word that could have been used is (مَتْرُوكًا) which means 'they left the Quran'. Allah didn't use the word (مَتْرُوكًا) because this word merely means 'they left the Quran'; the word (مَهْجُورًا) means 'they left the Quran *far* behind'. They were not close to the Quran, they migrated further away from the Quran, and they left it a long way behind them.

This however does not only include those who never used to recite the Quran. It also includes those who recited the Quran in this world but they never had the particular character that the Quran wants them to have. If you are reciting the Quran but you don't cultivate the character that Allah wants you to have, then this is also considered to be 'leaving the Quran far behind'. This is why, in the very same Surah in which this verse is mentioned, the last ruku (part) of Surah Furqan, Allah describes in great detail the kind of character He wants from us. So when Allah used the word (مَهْجُورًا) He was precise in choosing the right word.

Another amazing example which I find is where Allah talks about staying far away from adultery in the following verse:

وَلَا تَقْرَبُواْ ٱلزِّنَىٰٓ إِنَّهُ كَانَ فَٰحِشَةً وَسَآءَ سَبِيلاً

Nor come nigh to adultery: for it is a shameful (deed) and an evil, opening the road (to other evils). (Quran 17:32)

If you look at the words that Allah uses in this verse, Allah says: (وَلَا تَقْرَبُواْ ٱلزِّنَىٰٓ) which means 'do not go close to adultery'. Allah could have said: (وَلاَ تَزْنُوْا) which means 'don't commit adultery' which is more of a direct command, but He did not. Allah said: (وَلَا تَقْرَبُواْ ٱلزِّنَىٰ) do not go close to adultery, which means do not even go close to those things which will lead you to adultery, i.e looking at non-mahram, maintaining the hijab etc. So when Allah chose the word (وَلَا تَقْرَبُواْ ٱلزِّنَىٰٓ) He was right in choosing the perfect word.

Another example of the perfect choice of words is in the following verses. Allah says:

وَمَن يَعْمَلْ سُوٓءًا أَوْ يَظْلِمْ نَفْسَهُۥ ثُمَّ يَسْتَغْفِرِ ٱللَّهَ يَجِدِ ٱللَّهَ غَفُورًا رَّحِيمًا

If anyone does evil or wrongs his own soul but afterwards seeks Allah's forgiveness, he will find Allah Oft-Forgiving, Most Merciful. (Quran 4:110)

A similar message is repeated in another verse of the Quran, Allah says:

وَٱلَّذِينَ إِذَا فَعَلُواْ فَٰحِشَةً أَوْ ظَلَمُوٓاْ أَنفُسَهُمْ

And those who having done something to be ashamed of, or wronged their own souls. (Quran: 3:135)

When you look deeply at these two verses, we question why Allah uses 'or' between 'when someone does evil', and 'injustice to their soul'? Why separate 'committing a sin' from 'injustice to the soul'? Isn't committing a sin an injustice to our souls? Yes of course it is, so why separate both?

The answer to this is that sin, in and of itself, is evil, there is no doubt about that. Theft, adultery, and so forth are all evil acts, and they are surely injustices to our soul; but why did Allah differentiate between 'injustice to your soul' and 'committing a sin'? They are separated because when someone sins the purpose behind the sinning is pleasure. For instance, when someone steals, he is stealing because of pleasure, love of wealth, love of money and so on. When Allah separated 'Injustice to your soul', Allah is referring to those sins in which there is no pleasure. Sins that will neither benefit you in this world nor in the Hereafter. For example, being a witness to a false testimony is a sin, for such a crime as a punishment in this world you may get fined, and in the worst case you could be sent to prison *if you are caught*. So such a sin, neither benefits you in this world nor in the Hereafter, because for such a sin there is punishment in the Hereafter too. Unless the sinner repents or if Allah wishes He may forgive. So (فَٰحِشَةً) is a sin in which a sinner benefits and derives pleasure from it in this world, and gets punished in the Hereafter. (ظلم) Injustice to your soul is a sin from which the sinner does not benefit neither in this world nor in the Hereafter.

Singular and Plural Nouns

There are certain places in the Quran where Allah uses plural instead of singular nouns. Some critics of Islam have suggested these are mistakes in the Quran. These people fail to realise that this is not a mistake but a miracle, as you will see. An example of this is the following verse. Allah says:

كَذَّبَتْ قَوْمُ لُوطٍ ٱلْمُرْسَلِينَ

The people of Lut rejected the messengers. (Quran 26:160)

The people of Lut rejected Prophet Lut ﷺ, but Allah used a plural and said 'messengers', although Lut ﷺ was the only Prophet at that time. The question therefore is why did Allah use the plural (messengers) instead of the singular (messenger), because the people of Lut ﷺ only rejected him and not all the messengers?

The answer to this is that all the messengers that came, from Adam ﷺ to Prophet Muhammad ﷺ, preached one message, and that was the oneness of Allah. So because all the messengers preached one message, when the people of Lut rejected one messenger, (Lut), they indirectly rejected all the messengers, because all of the messengers' main message was the same, Tawheed i.e. the oneness of Allah.

There are certain verses in the Quran where Allah uses a singular form and a plural form in the same verse. Allah says:

ٱللَّهُ وَلِيُّ ٱلَّذِينَ ءَامَنُوا۟ يُخْرِجُهُم مِّنَ ٱلظُّلُمَٰتِ إِلَى ٱلنُّورِ

Allah is the Protector of those who believe. He brings them out from darkness into light. (Quran 2:257)

The word (ظُلُمَٰتِ - darknesses) is plural but the word (نُور - light) is singular. Why did Allah use plural and singular in this verse? The reason why Allah used plural for (ظُلُمَٰتِ) is because the paths of falsehood that lead to darkness are many, but there is only one path that is the true path, that will lead you to the light i.e. Paradise that's why Allah used the plural form for (ظُلُمَٰتِ) and used the singular form for (نُورٍ).

Semantics in the Quran

In this part you will study some of the examples as to why Allah uses two different words in different places, when they both have the same meaning.

One of the most amazing examples that I find in the Quran is the use of these two words: (امرأة – woman) and (زوجة – wife). Allah uses both of these to refer to a wife in the Quran. For instance, look at the following verses. Allah says:

وَمِنْ ءَايَٰتِهِ أَنْ خَلَقَ لَكُم مِّنْ أَنفُسِكُمْ أَزْوَٰجًا لِّتَسْكُنُوٓاْ إِلَيْهَا

And among His Signs is this; that He created for you wives from among yourselves, that you may find repose in them (Quran 30:21)

Allah uses the word (أَزْوَٰجًا) here, meaning wives. Here is another verse where He uses the same word:

رَبَّنَا هَبْ لَنَا مِنْ أَزْوَٰجِنَا وَذُرِّيَّٰتِنَا قُرَّةَ أَعْيُنٍ وَٱجْعَلْنَا لِلْمُتَّقِينَ إِمَامًا

Our Lord! Bestow on us from our wives and our offspring the comfort of our eyes, and make us leaders for the God fearing people. (Quran 25:74)

If you read Surah Tahreem, Allah talks about the wives of the Prophets Lut ﷺ and Nuh ﷺ, and Allah does not use the word (زوجة). He uses the word (امرأة) which literally means woman, although He is still referring to their wives:

ضَرَبَ ٱللَّهُ مَثَلًا لِّلَّذِينَ كَفَرُواْ ٱمْرَأَتَ نُوحٍ وَٱمْرَأَتَ لُوطٍ

Allah sets forth, as an example to the Unbelievers, the wife of Nuh and the wife of Lut (Lot): (Quran 66:10)

Why does Allah sometimes use the word (امرأة) and at other times use the word (زوجة)?

Then we look further and find something even more interesting. We find that Allah uses both of these words, (امرأة) and (زوجة) in different places when He is referring to the wife of Zakariyya ﷺ. Allah says, referring to the wife of Zakariyya ﷺ:

$$\text{وَكَانَتِ ٱمْرَأَتِى عَاقِرًا}$$

When my wife is barren (Quran 19:8)

In this verse, Allah uses the word (امرأة) to refer to Zakariyah's ﷺ wife but in another place, Allah refers to his wife as (زوجة):

$$\text{وَأَصْلَحْنَا لَهُ زَوْجَهُ}$$

We cured his wife's (barrenness) for him. (Quran 21:90)

Why does Allah sometimes use the word (امرأة) and sometimes use the word (زوجة)?

The reason why Allah uses these two words both referring to 'wife' is because there are two types of husband and wife relationship. The first type of relationship is based on religion. The Quran refers to the woman as a Muhsana - a fortress against the Shaitan because a righteous woman, by marrying a man, helps him keep to the path of rectitude in his life.

In the example of Lut ﷺ and Nuh ﷺ, Allah refers to their wives as (امرأة), which literally means woman. So Allah is telling us that a wife who does not bring her husband closer to Allah and his Prophet ﷺ does not deserve to be called a wife; she deserves to be called a woman. That is why in Surah Lahab, Allah refers to Abu Lahab's wife as (امرأة). She also distanced her husband from Allah.

The other type of relationship is based on children. Before Zakariyah ﷺ had a child, Allah referred to his wife as (امرأة), but after Allah granted him a child, Allah referred to her as (زوجة). In other words, you are not a complete family unless you have children. When you get married and you have a wife, fine you are married, but when you have a child then you are a complete family. This is why Allah uses the words (امرأة) and (زوجة) in different places. They differentiate between types of relationship.

The Mercy of Allah with the Believers

Another example are the following two verses. Allah says:

رَبَّنَآ أَفْرِغْ عَلَيْنَا صَبْرًا

Our Lord! Pour out constancy on us. (Quran 2:250)

فَصَبَّ عَلَيْهِمْ رَبُّكَ سَوْطَ عَذَابٍ

Therefore did thy Lord pour on them a scourge of diverse chastisement: (Quran 89:13)

Both (أَفْرِغْ) and (صَبَّ) means to pour. Specifically, (أَفْرِغْ) means to pour gently, without force, and this is pouring for the believers, meaning, O' Allah, when You pour constancy upon believers be gentle, don't pour it with force. In the second verse Allah used the word (صَبَّ) which also means to pour, but this is pouring with force, gushing, and this is directed at the non-believers, meaning Allah will pour the punishment on them with force.

Descriptions of the Earth

Allah gives two different descriptions of the Earth in the Quran. Let's look at the following two verses and then the explanation for why Allah has done this. Allah says:

وَتَرَى ٱلْأَرْضَ هَامِدَةً فَإِذَآ أَنزَلْنَا عَلَيْهَا ٱلْمَآءَ ٱهْتَزَّتْ وَرَبَتْ وَأَنبَتَتْ مِن كُلِّ زَوْجٍ بَهِيجٍ

And (further), thou seest the Earth barren and lifeless, but when We pour down rain on it, it is stirred (to life), it swells, and puts forth every kind of beautiful growth (in pairs). (Quran 22:5)

Allah describes the earth in another place:

وَمِنْ ءَايَٰتِهِۦ أَنَّكَ تَرَى ٱلْأَرْضَ خَٰشِعَةً فَإِذَآ أَنزَلْنَا عَلَيْهَا ٱلْمَآءَ ٱهْتَزَّتْ وَرَبَتْ إِنَّ ٱلَّذِىٓ أَحْيَاهَا

لَمُحْىِ ٱلْمَوْتَىٰٓ إِنَّهُۥ عَلَىٰ كُلِّ شَىْءٍ قَدِيرٌ

And among His Signs is this: Thou seest the Earth barren and desolate; but when We send down rain to it, it is stirred to life and yields increase. Truly, He Who gives to the (dead) Earth can surely give life to (men) who are dead. For He has power over all things. (Quran: 41:39)

In the first verse Allah describes the Earth as (هَامِدَةً) which means 'barren', in the second verse Allah describes the Earth as (خَٰشِعَةً) which also means 'barren'. In both verses the point is exactly the same, so why did Allah use two different words to describe the Earth as barren?

The first verse is from Surah Hajj, and the context of this verse is that the first part of this verse talks about the development of a human being. Towards the end of this verse Allah gives the example of a barren area of Earth, that He is the One Who gives life to the barren Earth.

The context of the second verse is that few verses before this verse talks about worshipping Allah alone and not worshipping the Sun and the Moon. Allah says:

وَمِنْ ءَايَٰتِهِ ٱلَّيْلُ وَٱلنَّهَارُ وَٱلشَّمْسُ وَٱلْقَمَرُ لَا تَسْجُدُواْ لِلشَّمْسِ وَلَا لِلْقَمَرِ وَٱسْجُدُواْ لِلَّهِ ٱلَّذِى

خَلَقَهُنَّ إِن كُنتُمْ إِيَّاهُ تَعْبُدُونَ

Among His Signs are the Night and the Day, and the Sun and the Moon. Adore not the Sun and the Moon, but adore Allah Who created them if it is Him ye wish to serve. (Quran 41:37)

Here the context is about salah and worship. In the context of worship, Allah uses the word (خَٰشِعَةً), the reason for this is because it is (خُشُوع – humbleness) that is expected from a believer in his salah, and in his worship and manner before Allah, and the word (خَٰشِعَةً) comes from (خُشُوع). That is why there was no need to complete the second verse with (وَأَنبَتَتْ مِن كُلِّ زَوْجٍ بَهِيجٍ) 'and puts forth every kind of beautiful growth' unlike the first verse, because the context here (in the second verse) is worshipping Allah.

Kindness to Parents

Another amazing verse that I find in the Quran is where Allah talks about being good and kind to your parents. He says:

وَوَصَّيْنَا ٱلْإِنسَٰنَ بِوَٰلِدَيْهِ حَمَلَتْهُ أُمُّهُ وَهْنًا عَلَىٰ وَهْنٍ وَفِصَٰلُهُ فِى عَامَيْنِ أَنِ ٱشْكُرْ لِى وَلِوَٰلِدَيْكَ إِلَىَّ ٱلْمَصِيرُ

And We have enjoined on man (to be good) to his parents: in travail upon travail did his mother bear him, and in years twain was his weaning: (hear the command) Show gratitude to Me and to thy parents: to Me is (thy final) Goal. (Quran 31:14)

At the beginning of the verse Allah commands us to be good to parents, i.e mother and father: He uses the word (وَٰلِدَيْهِ) which means parents. Towards the end of this verse, Allah again commands us to be grateful to parents, and Allah uses the word (وَٰلِدَيْكَ) which means your parents. However in the middle part of the verse, Allah talks about the merits of the mother, that your mother bore you for nine months, she was the one who fed you, she took care of you and so on. What about the father? Why did Allah talk about the merits of the mother but at the beginning and the end He commanded us to be good and kind to parents? Why didn't Allah mention the merits of the father?

A child can see very easily what their father did for them, like paying for education, paying for clothes food, and so forth. A child, as he grows up, he sees all these merits of his father, and does not forget them. The mother carries the child for nine months, feeds the child, and looks after him. How many of us can remember our mothers' taking care of us when we were small? As we grow up, we easily forget what our mothers have done for us. That is why Allah specifically mentions the merits of our mothers and not of fathers.

The Weakness of a Human Being

Allah describes how weak we human beings are when faced with His punishment, telling us we are so weak that we cannot bear it. So Allah illustrates the weakness of a human being by comparing it to the least and lightest punishment of His:

وَلَئِن مَّسَّتْهُمْ نَفْحَةٌ مِّنْ عَذَابِ رَبِّكَ لَيَقُولُنَّ يَٰوَيْلَنَآ إِنَّا كُنَّا ظَٰلِمِينَ

If but a breath of the Wrath of thy Lord do touch them they will then say:
"Woe unto us! We did wrong, indeed!" (Quran 21:46)

Firstly Allah describes this by saying (وَلَئِن) 'and if'. Allah did not say (إِذَا) which means 'when'. If Allah said 'when' it would mean 'it *will* happen', but Allah said 'if' meaning something which may or may not happen. In other words, 'if' is a lower level of occurance than 'when'. So Allah is saying if a breath of the punishment of your Lord were to touch you, then ...

Secondly, Allah uses the word (مَّسَّتْهُمْ) which means 'it touches them'. Allah did not say (أَصَابَهُمْ) which means 'it reaches them', he said (مَّسَّتْهُمْ) because this is the lowest level of something reaching someone and the lightest level of touch, so Allah is saying 'just a touch', or 'a very light touch'.

Then Allah says (نَفْحَةٌ) which means 'a breath'. Allah did not say (مَّسَّتْهُمُ العَذَاب) that 'a punishment touches them'. Allah used the word (نَفْحَةٌ) which means 'breath' to show the lightness of the punishment, meaning a minor and trivial level of punishment.

Then Allah uses the word (مِنْ), which is used for division and partition. Here it means 'part of the punishment'. Allah did not say (نَفْحَةٌ العَذَاب), Allah added (مِنْ) to show that just a part of Allah's punishment was to touch them.

Then Allah says (رَب) to show that He is the most merciful. This is followed by (كَ) which means 'you', referring to Muhammad ﷺ, who is also merciful.

Allah is describing to us the lowest level of punishment, and if you human beings cannot bear this lowest level of punishment, then how can you bear the punishment of the Hell? When you cannot bear the punishment of the Hell then how much more should you ask Allah to protect you from the punishment of the Hell? May Allah protect us all from His punishment. (Ameen)

Miracle of Repetition in Words

Allah uses certain words in the Quran in which the repetition of letters indicates repetition of the action. Here are some examples in the Quran. In Surah Nas, the last Surah, Allah says:

قُلْ أَعُوذُ بِرَبِّ ٱلنَّاسِ (١) مَلِكِ ٱلنَّاسِ (٢) إِلَهِ ٱلنَّاسِ (٣) مِن شَرِّ ٱلْوَسْوَاسِ ٱلْخَنَّاسِ (٤) ٱلَّذِى يُوَسْوِسُ فِى صُدُورِ ٱلنَّاسِ (٥) مِنَ ٱلْجِنَّةِ وَٱلنَّاسِ

Say: I seek refuge with the Lord and Cherisher of Mankind, The King (or Ruler) of Mankind– The God (or Judge) of Mankind– From the mischief of the Whisperer (of Evil), who withdraws (after his whispers)– (The same) who whispers into the hearts of Mankind – Among Jinns and among Men. (Quran 114:1-6)

Allah uses the word (يُوَسْوِسُ) in this surah. If you analyse this word, you will notice that it has repeated letters (وس/وس). The scholars say that this repetition indicates repetition of the action. In other words, Allah is saying that the Shaitan does not only whisper once and then he is done, (by using repetition in the letters) Allah is saying that the Shaitan whispers many times. He is constantly whispering to you and trying his best to misguide you and take you away from the straight path of Allah.

Further, if you analyse Allah did not say that the 'Shaitan puts whispers', He said 'he whispers', indicating that whispering is a very light action, it is not a strong or a heavy action of the Shaitan. Contrast that with: (خَنَّاس) 'one who withdraws after whispering'. Here, Allah did not repeat letters in this word, why? Because the Shaitan will only withdraw after whispering *once you remember Allah*. The moment you remember Allah the Shaitan will withdraw. So that's why Allah used (وس/وس) for when the Shaitan whispers, because he is constantly whispering; and used (خَنَّاس) without repetition of letters to show you that not everyone remembers Allah, and as a result, the Shaitan is not constantly withdrawing.

Another example of the repetition of letters is the first verse of Surah Zilzal. Allah says:

$$\text{إِذَا زُلْزِلَتِ ٱلْأَرْضُ زِلْزَالَهَا}$$

When the Earth is shaken to her (utmost) convulsion, (Quran 99:1)

This is another example of the repetition of letters (زل/زل) which shows repetition of the action, i.e. the Earth shakes more than once, it keeps on occurring. The Earth continues to shake during the Earthquake.

Miracles in the Vowel Signs

We have looked at the miracles in certain letters, but when we read the Quran diligently we will see that there are also miracles in the vowel signs. In this section you will be introduced to these vowel signs and the message that is conveyed through these vowel signs.

The first example is of a vowel sign called (Tashdeed), Allah says:

$$\text{وَلْيَطَّوَّفُواْ بِٱلْبَيْتِ ٱلْعَتِيقِ}$$

and (again) circumambulate the Ancient House." (Quran 22:29)

Allah did not say (وَلْيَطُوفُواْ), He said (وَلْيَطَّوَّفُواْ). When you circumambulate the ka'abah, seven circuits are required. If Allah had said (وَلْيَطُوفُواْ) then one circuit would have been sufficient, but (وَلْيَطَّوَّفُواْ) indicates that more than one circuit is required when you circumambulate the ka'abah.

Another example is found in the story of Yusuf ﷺ. When the women of the city (in Egypt) saw Yusuf's beauty ﷺ, Allah describes what they did. He says:

$$\text{فَلَمَّا رَأَيْنَهُ أَكْبَرْنَهُ وَقَطَّعْنَ أَيْدِيَهُنَّ}$$

So when they saw him, they found him great, and (were so stunned that they) cut their hands (Quran 12:31)

Allah didn't say (وَقَطَّعْنَ - and they cut their hands). Allah said: (وَقَطَّعْنَ - and they continued to cut their hands). The women of the city cut their hands, again and again. What was the reason that they kept cutting their hands? It was Yusuf's incredible beauty ﷺ. Allah is describing a scene for us in the Quran of Yusuf's beauty ﷺ by telling us that the women kept on cutting their hands.

As we read the Quran, we find other vowel signs in which messages are conveyed through these vowel signs. The following example is of a vowel sign called the (~ – Madd), Allah says:

وَمَآ أَرْسَلْنَاكَ إِلَّا كَآفَّةً لِّلنَّاسِ بَشِيرًا وَنَذِيرًا وَلَٰكِنَّ أَكْثَرَ ٱلنَّاسِ لَا يَعْلَمُونَ

We have not sent thee but as a (Messenger) to men, giving them Glad tidings, and warning them (against sin), but most men understand not. (Quran 34:28)

In the Arabic language there are two words that are used for 'All'. One is (كَآفَّةً) and the other is (جَمِيْعًا) and both of these words are used in the Quran. In this verse Allah did not say (جَمِيْعًا), but (كَآفَّةً), and there is a (~ – Madd) on the letter (ك), to encompass the entire world. Allah used the right word in this verse to tell us that Muhammad ﷺ was sent for the whole of mankind, not only for the Arabs of his time, but for his time, for today and for all people until the Day of Judgement.

Using Two Different Tenses for the Same Event

We find in the Quran that sometimes Allah uses two different tenses for the same event that has occurred. To illiustrate this I want to share with you two dreams that are popular in the Quran. Allah talks about the dreams that Yusuf ﷺ and Ibrahim ﷺ had in two different places in the Quran. Let us first look at what Allah said, and then we will discuss the tenses used in each of the verses. Allah says:

إِذْ قَالَ يُوسُفُ لِأَبِيهِ يَٰٓأَبَتِ إِنِّي رَأَيْتُ أَحَدَ عَشَرَ كَوْكَبًا

Behold Joseph said to his father: "O my father! I did see eleven stars" (Quran 12:4)

When Allah talks about the dream of 'Ibrahim' ﷺ, He says:

$$\text{قَالَ يَٰبُنَىَّ إِنِّ أَرَىٰ فِى ٱلۡمَنَامِ أَنِّ أَذۡبَحُكَ}$$

> He (Ibrahim) said, "O my little son, I have seen in a dream that I am slaughtering you" (Quran 37:102)

In both of these two verses, you can see that Allah in the first verse uses the word (رَأَيۡتُ) which means 'I saw', but in the second verse Allah uses the word (أَرَىٰ) which means 'I see'. Why did Allah use two different tenses when describing the dreams of both of these Prophets? Some people may say, 'they both mean the same and it's the same thing'. This is not true, had they both carried the same meaning, Allah would have used the same word in both places. So let us look at why Allah used different tenses in each place.

In the story of Yusuf ﷺ, using (رَأَيۡتُ - I saw), means there was only one 'seeing': he saw this dream only once. In the story of Ibrahim ﷺ Allah used the word (أَرَىٰ) which is used for repetition, i.e. Ibrahim ﷺ dreamt of this more than once. Thus the use of different tenses for the same event.

We further find in the Quran certain verses in which two different tenses are used in the same verse. Allah says:

$$\text{أَتَىٰٓ أَمۡرُ ٱللَّهِ فَلَا تَسۡتَعۡجِلُوهُ}$$

> The affair of Allah has come, so seek not to hasten it (Quran 16:1)

"The affair of Allah has come". This is a past tense, but it is followed by "do not hasten it". Why does Allah say not to hasten it when it has already come?

This is an illustration of the eloquence of the Arabic language. It tells us that 'the affair of Allah', i.e the Day of Judgement, will come with so much certainty that there can be no doubt about it. It is so certain that it is as if the Day of Judgement has already happened. When something has happened can it be stopped? No, once it has come it cannot be undone. So by using a past tense, Allah is emphasising the certainty of the coming of the Day of Judgement.

Omitting Pronouns

Another fascinating example I find in the Quran is when Allah omits pronouns. When Ibrahim ﷺ talks about Allah, and he says:

وَٱلَّذِى هُوَ يُطْعِمُنِى وَيَسْقِينِ (٧٩) وَإِذَا مَرِضْتُ فَهُوَ يَشْفِينِ (٨٠) وَٱلَّذِى يُمِيتُنِى ثُمَّ يُحْيِينِ

And it is **He** Who gives me food and drink. And when I am ill, it is **He** Who cures me; Who will cause me to die, and then to live (again); (Quran 26:79-81)

For feeding and drinking Allah uses (هُوَ - He). Also when He speaks about Ibrahim ﷺ being ill and being cured, He uses (هُوَ - He), but when Allah speaks about life and death, He does not use the word (هُوَ - He). Why?

When a person thinks about eating and drinking, then his mind can easily turn towards a provider other than Allah, i.e 'it was my earnings that paid for my food', or 'a kind and generous person I met' is the one who fed me and gave me to drink. Similarly, when a person goes to a doctor, his mind can easily imagine 'it is the doctor who has cured me.' So Allah, to emphasize this point that eating and drinking, and the cure for illness, is not from your earnings, is not from a human being and that it is only from Allah, He uses the word (هُوَ). But when we speak of life and death, even a non-beiever would say that it is God who gives life and death, so there was no need to emphasize this point with the word (هُوَ), and therefore there was no need to repeat the pronoun.

Answers to the Alleged 'Contradictions'

When we read the Quran, we find that it contains certain verses that seem to contradict other verses. This is due to lack of understanding. The Quran will never contradict itself, since it is from Allah. Let's look at some of these alleged contradictions in the Quran. Allah says:

وَلَيَحْمِلُنَّ أَثْقَالَهُمْ وَأَثْقَالاً مَّعَ أَثْقَالِهِمْ وَلَيُسْئَلُنَّ يَوْمَ ٱلْقِيَٰمَةِ عَمَّا كَانُواْ يَفْتَرُونَ

They will bear their own burdens, and (other) burdens along with their own and on the Day of Judgement they will be called to account for their falsehoods. (Quran 29:13)

This verse seems to contradict the following verse, in no less than three different places: Surah Anam, Surah Fatir and Surah Najm, Allah says:

$$\text{وَلَا تَزِرُ وَازِرَةٌ وِزْرَ أُخْرَىٰ}$$

3

Nor can a bearer of burdens bear another's burden. (Quran 35:18)

How can both sets of meanings in the verses be true? In both places the context is 'sins'. Will they bear the burden of others' sins or will they not bear the burden of others' sins? There seems to be a contradiction between the two. So how do we understand these verses?

The answer is that the second verse refers to an individual who commits a sin. Of such a person Allah says:

$$\text{وَأَن لَّيْسَ لِلْإِنسَٰنِ إِلَّا مَا سَعَىٰ}$$

That man can have nothing but what he strives for; (Quran 53:39)

So a person who sins will not bear the burden of another person. However, when one person helps or misguides another person towards committing a sin, that first person may not be committing that sin himself, but by helping someone else to commit a sin or by misguiding them, they too will bear the burden of that sin on their shoulders. This is explained in the Quran in another place where Allah says:

$$\text{لِيَحْمِلُوٓاْ أَوْزَارَهُمْ كَامِلَةً يَوْمَ ٱلْقِيَٰمَةِ وَمِنْ أَوْزَارِ ٱلَّذِينَ يُضِلُّونَهُم بِغَيْرِ عِلْمٍ أَلَا سَآءَ مَا يَزِرُونَ}$$

Let them bear, on the Day of Judgment, their own burdens in full, and also (something) of the burdens of those without knowledge, whom they misled. Alas how grievous the burdens they will bear! (Quran 16:25)

So if a person commits a sin, he will not bear another person's burden on his shoulders, but if he misguides another person then he will carry his own sin as well as the sin of the one whom he misguided.

Summary

Today you have seen some examples of eloquence in the Quran. You have studied miracles in letters, in the precise choice of words being used, and miracles even in the vowel signs.

You have only studied a few of the hundreds and thousands of miracles that are in the Quran. The purpose is not to draw attention to every miracle in the Quran, but to raise your awareness of its miraculous nature.

Workshop

The quiz questions and the exercises are provided to further your understanding. Don't worry if you can't answer all of the questions in the quiz. Try your best to answer as many as you can. However, you should go back over the chapter to check your answers.

Quiz 3

1. Which part of the Quran is a miracle?
2. Give an example of the precise choice of words used in the Quran?
3. When Allah talks about wives in the Quran, sometimes He uses the word 'wife' and sometimes he uses the word 'woman'; why is this?
4. Why are 'sin' and 'injustice to the body' treated as two separate things?
5. What is the miracle of repetition within certain words? Give an example.
6. Why does Allah use the past tense for something that will happen in the future?

Miracle of the Structure of Sentences in the Quran

DAY 4

Order of Surahs in the Quran

When we look at the Surahs in the Quran, we find them in an order which is difficult for us to understand. They are not in chronological order because the first surah to be revealed was Surah 96, which is nearly at the end of the Quran. The opening surah is Surah Fatihah which was not the first Surah to be revealed. Neither are the Surahs in the Quran in size order because the shortest surah in the Quran is Surah 108 (Surah Al-Kauthar), which is not the final surah of the Quran. So, how were the Surahs ordered as we see them today?

Some scholars say 'the Companions of the Prophet ﷺ ordered the Surahs in the Quran this way,' and that we should just accept this order. Allah wanted the Surahs to be in this order and the evidence they give is that none of the Companions of the Prophet ﷺ objected to this order of the Surahs in the Quran, and this is a very strong evidence, because there were instances when the Companions of the Prophet ﷺ did object to things. For example, some Companions objected to writing down the verses of the Quran, but when it came to the ordering of the Surahs in the Quran, the fact that no Companion objected to this ordering is clear proof that this order of Surahs in the Quran is the Divine order. In order to prove this point, Allah says:

إِنَّ عَلَيْنَا جَمْعَهُ وَقُرْءَانَهُ

It is for Us to collect it and to promulgate it: (Quran 75:17)

All the Surahs in the Quran has a connection with the Surah before it and after it. Here are some examples that show that the ordering of the Surahs is by Divine disposition. There is a wisdom behind the situation of each Surah.

The Connection Between Surah Rahman and Surah Waqia'h

Let us look at the connection between Surah Rahman and Surah Waqi'ah. Surah Rahman deals with five main subjects:

1.   The greatness of the Quran;

2.   A list of Allah's favours;

3.   What happens to people who are ungrateful, i.e, judgement and Hell Fire.

4. What the people of Paradise will get, in other words there is a tour of Paradise.

5. There is also a tour of the highest Paradise.

Now let us look at the five main subjects of Surah Waqi'ah, which follows Surah Rahman. In Surah Waqi'ah, in reverse order, the five main subjects are:

1. The last topic is about the greatness of the Quran.

2. The second to last subject is about the amazing creation that Allah has created.

3. Then it talks about the Hell Fire.

4. Then it talks about Paradise.

5. Finally it talks about the highest Paradise.

What an amazing correlation between these two Surahs!

The Connection Between Surah Isra and Surah Kahf

Likewise there is a connection between Surah Isra and Surah Kahf. The first verse of Surah Isra is:

سُبْحَانَ الَّذِي أَسْرَىٰ بِعَبْدِهِ لَيْلًا مِنَ الْمَسْجِدِ الْحَرَامِ إِلَى الْمَسْجِدِ الْأَقْصَى

Glorious is He Who made his servant travel by night from Al-Masjid-ul-Haram to Al-Masjid-ul-Aqsa (Quran 17:1)

The first verse of Surah Kahf is:

الْحَمْدُ لِلَّهِ الَّذِي أَنْزَلَ عَلَىٰ عَبْدِهِ الْكِتَابَ

Praise belongs to Allah who has sent down the Book to His servant (Quran 18:1)

In the first verse of Surah Isra, Muhammad ﷺ travels to the Heavens to get the revelation. In the first verse of Surah Kahf, the revelation travels to Muhammad ﷺ.

There is also another connection between these two Surahs. Shirk is the greatest sin in Islam and there are two types of Shirk (Shirk is treating something/someone as equal with Allah). The first type of Shirk is exalting a created being up to the level of The Creator; the second type of shirk is bringing The Creator down to the level of a creature. Both of these are ways in which a person can 'associate partners' with Allah.

Surah Isra talks about the Jews, well, what is the problem with the Jews' faith? They brought The Creator down to the level of a creature, saying for instance, Allah is resting, fighting with a Prophet and losing, etc. So the last verse of this Surah says to the Jews:

$$\text{وَقُلِ ٱلْحَمْدُ لِلَّهِ ٱلَّذِى لَمْ يَتَّخِذْ وَلَدًا وَلَمْ يَكُن لَّهُ شَرِيكٌ فِى ٱلْمُلْكِ وَلَمْ يَكُن لَّهُ وَلِيٌّ مِّنَ ٱلذُّلِّ وَكَبِّرْهُ تَكْبِيرًا}$$

Say, "Praise belongs to Allah who has neither had a son, nor is there any partner to Him in His kingdom, nor is anyone (needed) to protect Him from (any) weakness. And proclaim His greatness, an open proclamation. (Quran 17:111)

On the other hand, Surah Kahf talks about the Christians, well, what is the problem with the faith of the Christians? They exalted a human creature, Jesus ﷺ, to the level of the Creator. So when Allah talks to the Christians in Surah Kahf, in the last verse Allah instructs Prophet Muhammad ﷺ as follows:

$$\text{قُلْ إِنَّمَا أَنَا بَشَرٌ مِّثْلُكُمْ يُوحَىٰ إِلَىَّ أَنَّمَا إِلَهُكُمْ إِلَهٌ وَأَحِدٌ فَمَن كَانَ يَرْجُواْ لِقَآءَ رَبِّهِ فَلْيَعْمَلْ عَمَلاً صَلِحًا وَلَا يُشْرِكْ بِعِبَادَةِ رَبِّهِ أَحَدًا}$$

Say, "Surely, I am but a human being like you; it is revealed to me that your God is the One God. So the one who hopes to meet his Lord must do righteous deeds and must not associate anyone in the worship of his Lord." (Quran 18:110)

This verse was emphasizing the point of not raising the Prophet ﷺ to the level of the Creator, which is the problem with the Christians as that is precisely what they did. So Allah is instructing the Prophet ﷺ to tell the people that he is a human being like themselves, and not make the same mistake the Christians made wiith Jesus ﷺ. Such amazing beauty in the connections between these Surahs!

There is also a third connection between these two Surahs. The last verse of Surah Isra says:

$$وَقُلِ ٱلْحَمْدُ لِلَّهِ$$

Say, "Praise belongs to Allah" (Quran 17:111)

Allah begins Surah Kahf by saying:

$$ٱلْحَمْدُ لِلَّهِ ٱلَّذِىٓ أَنزَلَ عَلَىٰ عَبْدِهِ ٱلْكِتَٰبَ$$

Praise belongs to Allah who has sent down the Book to His servant. (Quran 18:1)

In other words Allah is saying whether you praise Me or you don't praise Me, all praise belongs to Me.

Can any ordinary person create a book so perfect, with such miracles, with such connections between the chapters, when these Surahs were not revealed in chronological order and verses from each Surah were revealed in stages at different times? No wonder Allah says in the Quran that if we were to reveal this book before a mountain, even the mountains would not be able to bear the weight of it.

Reversal in Order

One of the most amazing types of miracle in the Quran is when Allah reverses the order. Some people may say, 'Well, it means the same thing when Allah reverses the order'. No, it does not mean the same thing. Had it held the same meaning, Allah would not have changed the order. Let's look at an example of such a reversal in order. Allah says:

$$وَلَا تَقْتُلُوٓا۟ أَوْلَٰدَكُم مِّنْ إِمْلَٰقٍ نَّحْنُ نَرْزُقُكُمْ وَإِيَّاهُمْ$$

And do not kill your children because of poverty – We will give provision to you, and to them (Quran 6:151)

In another verse of the Quran Allah reverses the order and He says:

وَلَا تَقْتُلُوٓاْ أَوْلَٰدَكُمْ خَشْيَةَ إِمْلَٰقٍ نَّحْنُ نَرْزُقُهُمْ وَإِيَّاكُمْ

Kill not your children for fear of want: We shall provide, sustenance for them as well as for you: (Quran 17:31)

If you look carefully at these verses you can see that the order of the key elements within the second clause of the second verse is reversed in comparison with the previous verse. Why does Allah reverse the order? Some people may say 'it is the same thing'. It is not the same thing. Let's look at each verse and see why the sequencing has been changed.

In the first verse Allah is talking about a person who is impoverished and in the second verse Allah is talking about one who is less poor. So in the first verse, which is in reference to someone who is very poor, Allah is saying that because you are so poor, We are the One Who provides for <u>you</u> and for <u>them</u> (your children).

In the second verse, which is in reference to one who is not so poor, but who fears poverty and that if he has more children he will not be able to afford their upbringing, or he will not be able to look after them adequately, so Allah uses the word (خَشْيَةَ) which means fear, i.e. fear of poverty. You don't suffer poverty now, but you fear poverty in the future. That is why Allah said that He will provide sustenance for <u>them</u> as well as for <u>you</u>, Allah mentioned 'them' first, because the fear is for future poverty for them and their children, and not for the present.

That is why in the first verse (مِنْ – because of) is used, for something that is present, in this case poverty, whereas in the second verse (خَشْيَةَ – fear of) is used, which refers to something that may happen in the future.

Another fascinating example that I find of a reversal in order is a where Allah says in several places in the Quran:

إِنَّ ٱللَّهَ غَفُورٌ رَّحِيمٌ

For Allah is Oft-Forgiving Most Merciful. (Quran 2:173)

This complementary pairing is repeated over fifty times in the Quran, that Allah is Oft-Forgiving, Most Merciful. However, there is one verse in the Quran where this order is reversed. Allah says in Surah Saba:

$$يَعْلَمُ مَا يَلِجُ فِي ٱلْأَرْضِ وَمَا يَخْرُجُ مِنْهَا وَمَا يَنزِلُ مِنَ ٱلسَّمَآءِ وَمَا يَعْرُجُ فِيهَا وَهُوَ ٱلرَّحِيمُ ٱلْغَفُورُ$$

He knows all that goes into the Earth, and all that comes out thereof; all that comes down from the sky and all that ascends thereto: and He is the Most Merciful, the Oft-Forgiving. (Quran 34:2)

Why did Allah reverse the order in this verse? Some may say it has the same meaning. No, it is not the same. When Allah reverses the order, there is a wisdom behind this alternation.

Let's first see why Allah generally mentions (غَفُورُ - Oft-Forgiving) before (رَحِيمُ - Most Merciful). The scholars say that if Allah does not forgive a person, what happens to that person is that he will be doomed and he will enter into Hell. If Allah forgives him, then where will he go? He will go to Paradise, because of His mercy.

Allah takes a person out of Hell, with forgiveness; then He tells us that entry to Paradise is due to His mercy. So why did Allah reverse the order in Surah Saba?

Ibn Al Qayim رحمة الله عليه says that the scholars say: 'In the Quran, knowledge is always linked with Allah's mercy.' If you want to be guided through knowledge then you need the mercy of Allah. Without His mercy, that knowledge is not useful for you. The following verses are a proof for what the scholars quoted:

$$وَلَقَدْ جِئْنَٰهُم بِكِتَٰبٍ فَصَّلْنَٰهُ عَلَىٰ عِلْمٍ هُدًى وَرَحْمَةً لِّقَوْمٍ يُؤْمِنُونَ$$

For We had certainly sent unto them a Book, based on knowledge, which We explained in detail— a guide and a mercy to all who believe. (Quran 7:52)

$$رَبَّنَا وَسِعْتَ كُلَّ شَىْءٍ رَّحْمَةً وَعِلْمًا$$

Our Lord! You comprehend all things in mercy and knowledge (Quran 40:7)

So, we see that there is a link between (عِلْم - Knowledge) and (رَحْمَةً - Mercy), and they go hand in hand with each other, i.e when knowledge is not linked with the mercy of Allah then it will lead to destruction. Nowadays people have advanced

63

their knowledge of technology, have built tall buildings, but they don't accept the truth (of the Quran). So knowledge needs mercy, otherwise they will be destroyed. We find in the verse of Surah Saba, Allah speaks about knowledge, and because knowledge is necessarily linked with the mercy of Allah, He reversed the order to (وَهُوَ ٱلرَّحِيمُ ٱلْغَفُورُ - and He is the Most Merciful, the Oft-Forgiving). As Allah was talking about knowledge, He wisely mentioned mercy first and then forgiveness. In the other verses, forgiveness is mentioned first and then mercy, because the topic is not knowledge. Glory be to Allah that the Quran is utterly free of superfluity or accident; that even the apparently most minute and least noticeable elements of its enormously detailed syntactic, rhetorical and narrative structure is deliberately weighted with a specific and relevant significance. There is absolutely nothing occurring in all of its vastness of forms and meanings that is unforeseen, casual, coincidental or left to chance.

Misunderstanding of Certain Verses

There are certain verses in the Quran that if you read the translation of them you may misunderstand them, because in Arabic some verbs are elided as a known and accepted device of poetical expressiveness in the Arabic language. Let us look at the following example. Allah says:

وَإِذَآ أَرَدْنَآ أَن نُّهْلِكَ قَرْيَةً أَمَرْنَا مُتْرَفِيهَا فَفَسَقُواْ فِيهَا فَحَقَّ عَلَيْهَا ٱلْقَوْلُ فَدَمَّرْنَٰهَا تَدْمِيرًا

And when We intend to destroy a town, We command its affluent people, then they commit sins therein, so that the word (punishment) is proved true against them: then We destroy them utterly. (Quran 17:16)

If a person does not know Arabic, he may think that Allah commands the affluent people to go and commit sins; it is as though Allah wants to punish them, so Allah commands them to sin and then He destroys them; but this meaning is impossible. How can Allah command evil? Allah says:

إِنَّ ٱللَّهَ لَا يَأْمُرُ بِٱلْفَحْشَآءِ أَتَقُولُونَ عَلَى ٱللَّهِ مَا لَا تَعْلَمُونَ

Allah never commands what is shameful: do ye say of Allah what ye know not? (Quran 7:28)

$$\text{إِنَّ ٱللَّهَ يَأْمُرُ بِٱلْعَدْلِ وَٱلْإِحْسَٰنِ}$$

Allah commands justice, the doing of good (Quran 16:90)

So Allah never commands sinning or evildoing. Therefore, the meaning has to be something else. In Arabic, as in many other literary languages, certain elements can be elided for eloquence. When Allah says that He intends to destroy a town, it is a town whose inhabitants are perpetrating injustice and wanton behaviour; whose inhabitants have transgressed and sinned. Allah will not destroy anyone or anything unless they deserve destruction, because Allah Himself is not unjust.

$$\text{إِنَّ ٱللَّهَ لَا يَظْلِمُ مِثْقَالَ ذَرَّةٍ}$$

Allah is never unjust in the least degree (Quran 4:40)

When Allah decides to destroy a city which deserves destruction because of the peoples' sins and injustice, Allah opens up the last door of repentance, and He orders them to repent their sins. So when Allah commands, He does not command them to sin; Allah commands them to repent before it is too late to do so. The people are told that a book has come to them, a messenger has come to them to warn them, to give them one last chance. If they still continue to sin, then destruction will come. So when Allah says, 'We command its affluent people', He does not command them to sin, He commands them to repent, to come back to the straight path. If they repent they will be saved, but if they continue in their transgressions and in their wrongdoings after the last chance has been given to them, then at that point destruction will come. So this verse shows both the justice and the mercy of Allah. Allah does not want to destroy the city, in His mercy He gives them repeated opportunities for repentance and warns in advance of the last chance.

There are other verses in the Quran that are open to misunderstanding due to their translations. If you are reading a translation and you don't quite understand it, refer to its commentary.

The Ease in the Month of Ramadhan

Allah talks about fasting in the Quran in Surah Baqarah. Allah says:

أَيَّامًا مَّعْدُودَٰتٍ فَمَن كَانَ مِنكُم مَّرِيضًا أَوْ عَلَىٰ سَفَرٍ فَعِدَّةٌ مِّنْ أَيَّامٍ أُخَرَ وَعَلَى ٱلَّذِينَ يُطِيقُونَهُ فِدْيَةٌ طَعَامُ مِسْكِينٍ فَمَن تَطَوَّعَ خَيْرًا فَهُوَ خَيْرٌ لَّهُ وَأَن تَصُومُوا۟ خَيْرٌ لَّكُمْ إِن كُنتُمْ تَعْلَمُونَ (١٨٤) شَهْرُ رَمَضَانَ ٱلَّذِىٓ أُنزِلَ فِيهِ ٱلْقُرْءَانُ هُدًى لِّلنَّاسِ وَبَيِّنَٰتٍ مِّنَ ٱلْهُدَىٰ وَٱلْفُرْقَانِ فَمَن شَهِدَ مِنكُمُ ٱلشَّهْرَ فَلْيَصُمْهُ وَمَن كَانَ مَرِيضًا أَوْ عَلَىٰ سَفَرٍ فَعِدَّةٌ مِّنْ أَيَّامٍ أُخَرَ يُرِيدُ ٱللَّهُ بِكُمُ ٱلْيُسْرَ وَلَا يُرِيدُ بِكُمُ ٱلْعُسْرَ

(Fasting) for a fixed number of days; but if any of you is ill or on a journey, the prescribed number (should be made up) from days later. For those who can do it (with hardship) is a ransom, the feeding of one that is indigent. But he that will give more of his own free-will—it is better for him, and it is better for you that ye fast, if ye only knew. Ramadan is the (month) in which was sent down the Quran as a guide to mankind also clear (Signs) for guidance and judgment (between right and wrong). So every one of you who is present (at his home) during that month should spend it in fasting, but if anyone is ill, or on a journey, the prescribed period (should be made up) by days later. Allah intends every facility for you He does not want to put you to difficulties. (Quran 2:184-185)

The word (مَّعْدُودَٰتٍ) refers to maximum number of 10 days. So in this verse Allah is referring to fasts before the fasting for the whole month of Ramadhan was made compulsory. Here Allah gives two options for those people who miss these fasts due to travelling or sickness. The first option is to feed the poor, and the second option is to make up for the missed fast. So you have <u>two</u> options, though Allah says that making up for your fast is the better option for you.

In the next verse, Allah talks about the month of Ramadhan. Allah says that when one witnesses this month, one should be sure to fast the entire month. He further says that if one were to miss fasts due to sickness or travelling, then there is only <u>one</u> option: and that is to make up for the missed fast.

So I would like to ask you, dear reader, did things get easier than before or more difficult? Things got more difficult, despite Allah saying that He wants to make things easy for you and not difficult. How can this be true, because we see that Allah made things more difficult? Well, first there were <u>10</u> compulsory days of fasting, then in the month of Ramadhan Allah commanded the believers to fast for the <u>entire</u> month, and this is much harder. Furthermore, if they missed their fasts, they had two options; but in the month of Ramadhan, if they were to miss a fast due to sickness or travelling, now they only have one option and that is to make up for the missed fast. How is this showing that Allah wants to make things easier for you?

The scholars answered this and said that when you fast a day outside the month of Ramadhan, it is ten times more difficult than to fast a day in the month of Ramadhan. Isn't this Allah making things easier for you?

Furthermore, Ramadhan is a month of discipline, so when Allah has restrained the Shaitans of temptation, opened up the doors of Paradise, closed the doors of Hell for you, then isn't it much easier for one to abstain from sin? When this is the case, then isn't this Allah making things easier for you?

4

Perfect Sentence Structure

Allah says in the Quran:

$$مَّا جَعَلَ ٱللَّهُ لِرَجُلٍ مِّن قَلْبَيْنِ فِى جَوْفِهِ$$

Allah has not made for any man two hearts in his (one) body: (Quran 33:4)

Allah used the word (رَجُلٍ) here, meaning a man. Allah specifically excluded women by using the word 'man', so someone may ask, does this mean that women can have two hearts?

When a woman becomes pregnant, and she carries a child in her womb, how many hearts does she have in her body? Two hearts: the heart of the child and her own heart. If she had twins then there will be three hearts in her body. So when Allah excluded women from this verse, Allah was accurate in excluding them.

Conciseness of Speech

When we read the Quran we see that Allah uses concise expressions in many places. This means that He uses the shortest phrase with the most meaningful sentence. There are many examples of conciseness of speech in the Quran.

One Word Contains the Entire Meaning of Obedience

Allah says:

$$\text{إِنَّ ٱلَّذِينَ قَالُوا۟ رَبُّنَا ٱللَّهُ ثُمَّ ٱسْتَقَـٰمُوا۟}$$

Verily, those who say: "Our Lord is Allah" and then they stand firm, (Quran 41:30)

The word (ٱسْتَقَـٰمُوا۟) contains the entire meaning of abstaining from sins, and not going astray. Just one word contains the entire meaning of obedience to Allah after *Iman*. In other words, when they said, "Our Lord is Allah," they believed, they knew there was only one Lord (monotheism), "and then they stood firm", this means that they did not deviate in their belief, or in their monotheism, or in obeying the laws of the Quran. This one word contains all of this in its meaning. Allah didn't need to list things separately, i.e. they stayed firm in belief, then they stayed firm in their monotheism, then they stayed firm in their rituals, then they stayed firm in their character and so forth. Just one word contains the entire meaning of obedience!

One Word Contains all Types of Contracts

Another example of concise speech is where Allah uses a certain word which contains all types of contracts.

$$\text{يَـٰٓأَيُّهَا ٱلَّذِينَ ءَامَنُوٓا۟ أَوْفُوا۟ بِٱلْعُقُودِ}$$

O you who believe, fulfill the contracts. (Quran 5:1)

Allah has given this instruction which is non-specific, meaning that whatever contract you bind yourself to, you must make sure you fulfil it. The biggest contract of all is the contract with Allah, the contract of salah, fasting, zakah, and so on. This one word also includes contracts concerning business transactions, contracts in the workplace, contracts between spouses. So Allah has given this general instruction; that any contract you enter into, you must make sure that you fulfil it. Allah is ordering us to fulfil all types of contracts in just two words.

Two Words Contain the Past and the Future

Let us look at another example of concise speech. Allah says in the Quran:

$$\text{أَلَآ إِنَّ أَوْلِيَآءَ ٱللَّهِ لَا خَوْفٌ عَلَيْهِمْ وَلَا هُمْ يَحْزَنُونَ}$$

Behold! Verily on the friends of Allah there is no fear, nor shall they grieve; (Quran 10:62)

Allah is telling us that when someone becomes a friend of His then that person has no fear, and they shall not grieve. Allah uses two words here, one is (خَوْفٌ – fear) and the other is (حَزَن – grief). Let us examine these words.

The word (خَوْفٌ – fear) specifically means fear of the future. You don't know what is going to happen tomorrow. You are worried about losing your job, you are worried about your children's education, and so forth. This fear is worrying about the future.

The word (حَزَن – grief) is to grieve over something that has happened in the past. Feeling hurt and pain for what happened yesterday, or mourning a loss that has happened.

So Allah says that His friends shall have no fear of the future and neither shall they grieve over what has happened in the past. Two words describing the past and the future.

Three Words Contain the Propagation of the Entire Religion

فَٱصْدَعْ بِمَا تُؤْمَرُ

So, proclaim what you are commanded to. (Quran 15:94)

Here Allah commands the Prophet ﷺ to propagate and proclaim the entire religion. This includes monotheism, the laws, the prohibitions and lawful acts, desired character traits etc. Allah didn't need to list things separately, everything that you have been commanded, Muhammad ﷺ was told to proclaim and propagate it.

The Signs of Allah

Allah talks about the greatness of His signs in the Quran.

وَٱلشَّمْسِ وَضُحَىٰهَا (١) وَٱلْقَمَرِ إِذَا تَلَىٰهَا (٢) وَٱلنَّهَارِ إِذَا جَلَّىٰهَا (٣) وَٱلَّيْلِ إِذَا يَغْشَىٰهَا (٤) وَٱلسَّمَآءِ وَمَا بَنَىٰهَا (٥) وَٱلْأَرْضِ وَمَا طَحَىٰهَا (٦) وَنَفْسٍ وَمَا سَوَّىٰهَا

I swear by the Sun and his broad light, and by the Moon when she follows him, and by the day when he shows his brightness, and by the night when it envelops him, and by the sky, and the One who built it, and by the Earth, and the One who spread it, and by the soul, and the One who made it well; (Quran 91:1-7)

Why is Allah talking about the Sun, the Moon, the day, the night, the sky, the Earth and so on? The reason is because every day we leave our homes, and we don't always consciously think about the Sun, we don't always think about the daylight, we don't think about the Earth or the sky, we take them all for granted. Allah is telling us that every one of these is a miracle from among His miracles.

Let me describe a scenario to you. Suppose a child never saw daylight for few years, and he was kept in total darkness. After few years he is taken out of this darkness into the light, and for the first time in his life he sees daylight. I want to ask you, wouldn't he be amazed? Wouldn't he be astonished when he sees this daylight? So, Allah is telling you, 'you think that these are small signs?' No. They are not small, these are great signs.

The Quran gives many examples that show the greatness of His signs. Allah says: (وَٱلَّيْلِ إِذَا يَغْشَىٰ – I swear by the night when it covers (the Sun)); (وَٱلضُّحَىٰ – I swear by the morning light); (وَٱلتِّينِ وَٱلزَّيْتُونِ – I swear by the Fig and the Olive); and (وَٱلْعَصْرِ – I swear by the Time); all these are mentioned to show you the greatness of His signs.

The Greatness of the Water that you Drink

Allah describes to us the greatness of water, and His signs that are there in the water when you drink, Allah says:

أَفَرَءَيْتُمُ ٱلْمَآءَ ٱلَّذِى تَشْرَبُونَ (٦٨) ءَأَنتُمْ أَنزَلْتُمُوهُ مِنَ ٱلْمُزْنِ أَمْ نَحْنُ ٱلْمُنزِلُونَ (٦٩) لَوْ نَشَآءُ جَعَلْنَٰهُ أُجَاجًا فَلَوْلَا تَشْكُرُونَ

See ye the water which ye drink? Do ye bring it Down (in rain) from the Cloud or do We? Were it Our Will, We could make it salt (and unpalatable): then why do ye not give thanks? (Quran 56:68-70)

Water itself is a miracle. Allah has created every living thing from water. Have you ever drunk water mindfully, aware that you are drinking a miracle? Next time you hold a glass of water in your hands, imagine that you are holding a miracle of Allah in your hands.

These are all miracles that you probably don't ponder over, and probably don't reflect upon, and the Quran is reminding you over and over again, pointing these miracles out to you so that you increase your Iman and your obedience to Allah.

The Endings of Verses in the Quran

In the earlier part of the book I shared with you a story about 'Imam Ismaee' رحمة الله عليه, where he made a mistake and a person from the gathering stood up and corrected him. I want to share another example with you, which shows that even the endings of verses in the Quran are in the right places. Allah says:

وَإِن تَعُدُّواْ نِعْمَتَ ٱللَّهِ لَا تُحْصُوهَآ إِنَّ ٱلْإِنسَٰنَ لَظَلُومٌ كَفَّارٌ

If ye would count up the favours of Allah, never would ye be able to number them: Indeed, man is highly unjust, very ungrateful. (Quran 14:34)

وَإِن تَعُدُّواْ نِعْمَةَ ٱللَّهِ لَا تُحْصُوهَآ إِنَّ ٱللَّهَ لَغَفُورٌ رَّحِيمٌ

If ye would count up the favours of Allah, never would ye be able to number them: for Allah is Oft-Forgiving, Most Merciful. (Quran 16:18)

Look at these verses: both have the same beginning but each has a different ending. Why is this? Let us look at the context of these two verses to understand why the endings differ.

The context of the first verse is:

وَءَاتَىٰكُم مِّن كُلِّ مَا سَأَلْتُمُوهُ

And He gave you whatever you asked for. (Quran 14:34)

The context of the second verse is:

71

$$أَفَمَن يَخْلُقُ كَمَن لَّا يَخْلُقُ أَفَلَا تَذَكَّرُونَ$$

Is then He Who creates like one that creates not? Will ye not receive admonition? (Quran 16:17)

The subject of the first verse is human beings, the subject of the second verse is Allah. When Allah talked about human beings, He ended it with the fact that human beings are unjust and ungrateful. When Allah spoke of Himself, the ending was forgiveness and mercy.

The Companions of the Prophet ﷺ knew that the endings of these verses were designed. They realized that every single verse of the Quran ends in the correct way and with the most beautiful ending. Amongst the narrations in the Hadith we find that one of the Companions of the Prophet ﷺ by the name of Zayd Ibn Thabit ؓ, used to write down the revelation. The Prophet ﷺ used to dictate to him, and Zayd would carefully inscribe the words. So the Prophet ﷺ dictated the following verses:

$$وَلَقَدْ خَلَقْنَا ٱلْإِنسَٰنَ مِن سُلَٰلَةٍ مِّن طِينٍ (١٢) ثُمَّ جَعَلْنَٰهُ نُطْفَةً فِى قَرَارٍ مَّكِينٍ (١٣) ثُمَّ خَلَقْنَا ٱلنُّطْفَةَ عَلَقَةً فَخَلَقْنَا ٱلْعَلَقَةَ مُضْغَةً فَخَلَقْنَا ٱلْمُضْغَةَ عِظَٰمًا فَكَسَوْنَا ٱلْعِظَٰمَ لَحْمًا ثُمَّ أَنشَأْنَٰهُ خَلْقًا ءَاخَرَ$$

Man We did create from a quintessence (of clay); Then We placed him as (a drop of) sperm in a place of rest firmly fixed; (Then We made the sperm into a clot of congealed blood; then of that clot We made a (foetus) lump; then We made out of that lump bones and clothed the bones with flesh; then We developed out of it another creature: (Quran 23:12-14)

When the Prophet ﷺ reached this point, immediately 'Mua'adh Ibn Jabal' ؓ said:

$$فَتَبَارَكَ ٱللَّهُ أَحْسَنُ ٱلْخَٰلِقِينَ$$

So blessed be Allah, the Best to create! (Quran 23:14)

The Prophet ﷺ smiled. Mua'adh Ibn Jabal ؓ said: "O Prophet, why did you smile?" and the Prophet ﷺ replied: "Indeed the ending is:

فَتَبَارَكَ ٱللَّهُ أَحْسَنُ ٱلْخَلِقِينَ

So blessed be Allah, the Best to create! (Quran 23:14)"

This shows that the Companions understood the Quran. The Arabs understood the book of Allah, and this shows that every single verse in the Quran is ended in the most beautiful way; and this is amongst the many miracles of the Quran.

Summary

Today, you have learnt some of the miracles that the Quran has in the structure of its sentences. You studied how Allah uses conciseness of speech in the Quran, and why Allah reverses the order in certain verses of the Quran.

Remember the reasons why you are studying these miracles in the Quran. One reason we mentioned on Day 1 was to increase our Iman. When we ponder and reflect over these miracles a believer will only Glorify Allah and his obedience to Allah would increase.

Workshop

The quiz questions and the exercises are provided to further your understanding. Don't worry if you can't answer all of the questions in the quiz. Try your best to answer as many as you can. It is advisable to go back through the chapter to check your answers to these questions.

Quiz 4

1. In which order are the Surahs of the Quran organized?
2. Give an example of two verses in the Quran where the order of certain key elements is reversed. Give a reason behind this.
3. Give two examples of the conciseness of speech used in the Quran.

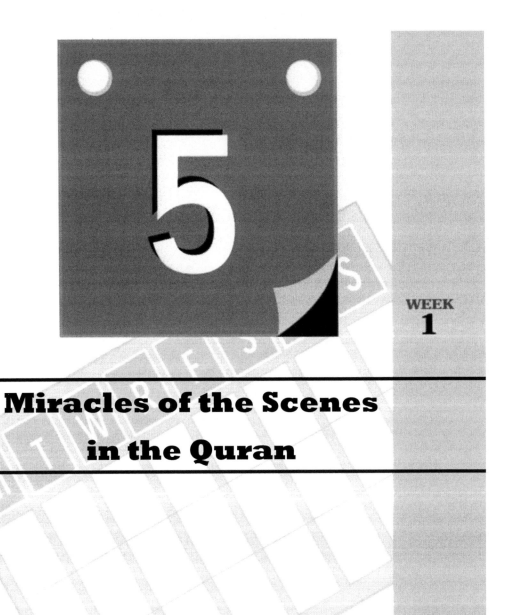

Miracles of the Scenes
in the Quran

DAY 5

Miracles of the Scenes in the Quran

Up until now you have studied miracles in the Quran based on language, style, eloquence, and word selection. There is another kind of miracle in the Quran and that is Allah describing scenes to us. For example, a lecturer may describe a scene for you, 'imagine you see a beautiful garden, with trees, roses and some other beautiful flowers.' The lecturer is painting a picture for his audience to imagine a scene. In the Quran, Allah has mentioned and described scenes to us so that we as humans can imagine what Allah wants us to see.

The early scholars of Islam wrote very little on this subject. One of the first scholars who did, and in great detail, was Sayyid Qutub. He was one of the first scholars who opened the doors on this topic, the miracles of the scene in the Quran.

I have found that when one starts to read the Quran one will find verse upon verse that paint pictures for us. On almost every page of the Quran one will read verses that are Quranic miracles of scenic description. In todays chapter you will look at some of these scenarios.

A Scene with Sinners

Allah describes to us the scene of sinners standing in front of Him on the Day of Judgement. Allah says:

وَلَوْ تَرَىٰٓ إِذِ ٱلْمُجْرِمُونَ نَاكِسُواْ رُءُوسِهِمْ عِندَ رَبِّهِمْ

> If only thou couldst see when the guilty ones will bend low their heads before their Lord, (Quran 32:12)

Allah describes how the sinners and the criminals will be standing and bending low their heads in front of Him on the Day of Judgement.

A Scene with Disbelievers

Allah tells us in the Quran that there is no chance for the disbelievers to enter Paradise. Those who reject the Quran, shall never enter Paradise: In fact, their entry into Paradise is impossible. These are the words of a human being, but now look at the description in the Quran of this fact:

$$\text{إِنَّ ٱلَّذِينَ كَذَّبُواْ بِـَٔايَـٰتِنَا وَٱسْتَكْبَرُواْ عَنْهَا لَا تُفَتَّحُ لَهُمْ أَبْوَٰبُ ٱلسَّمَآءِ وَلَا يَدْخُلُونَ ٱلْجَنَّةَ حَتَّىٰ}$$

$$\text{يَلِجَ ٱلْجَمَلُ فِى سَمِّ ٱلْخِيَاطِ}$$

Surely, those who have rejected Our signs and stood arrogant against them, the gates of the Heavens shall not be opened for them, and they shall not enter Paradise unless a camel passes through the eye of a needle. (Quran 7:40)

Allah is saying that until a camel passes through the eye of a needle those who rejected the signs of Allah will not enter Paradise. Can a camel ever go through the eye of a needle? Of course not! So, in the same way that it is impossible for the camel to go through the eye of a needle, it is impossible for those who have rejected the signs of Allah to enter Paradise. What an amazing scene is being described to us by Allah in the Quran.

A Scene of the Deeds of Non-Believers

Allah tells us that no matter how good the deeds of the non-believers may look, they are worthless, because there is no Iman. So due to the lack of Iman, no matter how good their deeds may look they will never be able to gather and count their good deeds. Let us look at how Allah describes this scene for us in the Quran:

$$\text{وَقَدِمْنَآ إِلَىٰ مَا عَمِلُواْ مِنْ عَمَلٍ فَجَعَلْنَـٰهُ هَبَآءً مَّنثُورًا}$$

And We shall turn to whatever deeds they did (in this life), and We shall make such deeds as floating dust scattered about. (Quran 25:23)

Allah is saying that He will make all the deeds that the non-believers did in this world as floating dust scattered about. Imagine if a person wanted to gather dust in the air and try to do something with it, is this possible? Allah describes their deeds on the Day of Judgement in this way to show that they will be worthless and even if they manage to gather something together, it will still be worthless and weightless.

The Quran gives another, very similar, example of the deeds of the non-believers. Allah says:

$$\text{مَّثَلُ ٱلَّذِينَ كَفَرُواْ بِرَبِّهِمْ أَعْمَـٰلُهُمْ كَرَمَادٍ ٱشْتَدَّتْ بِهِ ٱلرِّيحُ فِى يَوْمٍ عَاصِفٍ لَّا يَقْدِرُونَ مِمَّا كَسَبُواْ}$$

$$\text{عَلَىٰ شَىْءٍ}$$

The deeds of those who refuse to believe in their Lord are like ashes blown away by the wind on a stormy day. They will not be able to gain anything out of what they did. (Quran 14:18)

Allah is asking you to imagine someone trying to capture ashes as they are blown around by the wind on a stormy day. How far would one get? Nowhere at all. Similarly, the non-believers will get no benefit whatsoever from their deeds due to the lack of Iman. What an amazing scene given to us by Allah in this verse.

A Scene of Charity done by a Believer and a Non-Believer

I want to share another example with you, that of charity. Firstly, two illustrations of charity given by a believer, the first one who gives charity for the purpose of reminding others of his generosity, and the second one who gives charity for the pleasure of Allah. Then I want to share with you another type of charity, that given by a non-believer.

In the following verse Allah talks about the one who gives charity to seek the pleasure of Allah, he does not give charity for any worldy reason. Allah says:

وَمَثَلُ ٱلَّذِينَ يُنفِقُونَ أَمْوَٰلَهُمُ ٱبْتِغَآءَ مَرْضَاتِ ٱللَّهِ وَتَثْبِيتًا مِّنْ أَنفُسِهِمْ كَمَثَلِ جَنَّةٍ بِرَبْوَةٍ أَصَابَهَا وَابِلٌ فَآتَتْ أُكُلَهَا ضِعْفَيْنِ فَإِن لَّمْ يُصِبْهَا وَابِلٌ فَطَلٌّ وَٱللَّهُ بِمَا تَعْمَلُونَ بَصِيرٌ

The example of those who spend their wealth to seek the pleasure of Allah and to make firm (their faith) from (the depths of) their souls is like a garden on a height on which came a heavy rain, and it yielded its produce twofold. Even if a heavy rain does not come to it, a light drizzle is enough, and Allah is watchful of what you do. (Quran 2:265)

The charity of the one who gives to seek His pleasure is like a big garden with trees on a hill. When a heavy rain falls, the garden doubles its yield of fruit. Even if only a light rain falls, it will still give you fruit. This illustrates the charity of a believer. No matter how small the deed, as long as it is for the pleasure of Allah, it will bear fruit. All charity done with sincerity is great in the sight of Allah even if it is little.

You may only have $1 in your pocket, but when you spend that amount in charity, because you spent it with sincerity, seeking the pleasure of Allah, that $1 could have multiplied ten times or even more how ever much Allah wanted to multiply it.

Allah then describes the scene of a believer who gives charity but he always reminds others of his generosity:

يَٰٓأَيُّهَا ٱلَّذِينَ ءَامَنُوا۟ لَا تُبْطِلُوا۟ صَدَقَٰتِكُم بِٱلْمَنِّ وَٱلْأَذَىٰ كَٱلَّذِى يُنفِقُ مَالَهُ رِئَآءَ ٱلنَّاسِ وَلَا يُؤْمِنُ بِٱللَّهِ وَٱلْيَوْمِ ٱلْءَاخِرِ فَمَثَلُهُ كَمَثَلِ صَفْوَانٍ عَلَيْهِ تُرَابٌ فَأَصَابَهُ وَابِلٌ فَتَرَكَهُ صَلْدًا لَّا يَقْدِرُونَ عَلَىٰ شَىْءٍ مِّمَّا كَسَبُوا۟ وَٱللَّهُ لَا يَهْدِى ٱلْقَوْمَ ٱلْكَٰفِرِينَ

O you who believe, do not nullify your acts of charity by boasting about (doing people a) favour and by causing (them) hurt, like the one who spends his wealth to show off before people and does not believe in Allah and in the Last Day. So, his example is like a rock on which there is dust, then a heavy rain came over it and left it barren. They have no ability to gain anything out of what they have done, and Allah does not give guidance to the people who disbelieve. (Quran 2:264)

Allah tells us that the one who gives charity by reminding others of his generosity is like a hypocrite who does not believe in Allah and in the Hereafter. Allah describes him as a rock that has soil on top. Suppose you see a rock that has some soil on top of it; you would imagine something could grow on it when rain falls. Instead, when heavy rain falls, it washes away the soil leaving the stone barren, and nothing will grow on it. Allah is describing for us a hypocrite whose heart is like a stone. The soil in this scene represents Iman. They appear to be righteous, but in reality there is no Iman, no goodness, so Allah tells us not to be like such a person. When you give charity and you follow it by boasting of your favours and/or causing pain to people, you are like this hypocrite. Your deed appears to be righteous but in reality there is no goodness. Therefore don't tarnish your charity with reminders and hurt.

When next you give charity, keep both of these verses in mind, and give your charity purely for the sake of Allah so that your fruit yield is doubled.

In the following verse Allah describes for us the example of a non-believer who gives charity and his intention is to do good, Allah says:

مَثَلُ مَا يُنفِقُونَ فِى هَٰذِهِ ٱلْحَيَوٰةِ ٱلدُّنْيَا كَمَثَلِ رِيحٍ فِيهَا صِرٌّ أَصَابَتْ حَرْثَ قَوْمٍ ظَلَمُوٓاْ أَنفُسَهُمْ فَأَهْلَكَتْهُ

The likeness of that which they expend in this life of the world is as the likeness of a wind wherein is intense cold, it befalls the tilth of a people who have wronged themselves, and destroys it. (Quran 3:117)

Here Allah is describing for us the non-believers who practise charity. (صِرٌّ) is described as an extremely cold wind. So Allah tells us to imagine there is a young crop in a field, and before the fruits appeared, before the time came to harvest, a strong cold wind blew. What happened to the fruits that were to come? They were destroyed. This illustrates the futility of the charity of a non-believer: Allah will destroy their deeds on the Day of Judgement and their efforts will be worthless.

A Scene with One who Commits Shirk

Another amazing scene in the Quran is a description of one who associates partners with Allah. Allah says:

وَمَن يُشْرِكْ بِٱللَّهِ فَكَأَنَّمَا خَرَّ مِنَ ٱلسَّمَآءِ فَتَخْطَفُهُ ٱلطَّيْرُ أَوْ تَهْوِى بِهِ ٱلرِّيحُ فِى مَكَانٍ سَحِيقٍ

If anyone assigns partners to Allah it is as if he had fallen from Heaven and been snatched up by birds or the wind had swooped (like a bird on its prey) and thrown him into a far-distant place. (Quran 22:31)

Allah describes for us the fate of the one who commits shirk. One who regards something as equal with Allah. He is described as being like the one who fell from the Heaven, and before he reaches the Earth, a bird snatches him, or the winds blow him to a far distant place. We do not know where he ends up. Such a person has no end. This is how it is for the one who associates partners with Allah, though there is no end of him, his fate does not bear thinking about.

A Scene with One to Whom Knowledge is Accessible but who Never Took Advantage of it

Allah describes for us the condition of people for whom knowledge and education were easily accessible, but they never availed themselves of that knowledge. For example, a teenager who was brought up in a pious family, or in a house of scholars so knowledge was easily accessible to him. Or a person who lives in an Islamic environment, where there are Islamic lectures and circles of knowledge, and that knowledge is easily accessible to him, but he does not listen, or study, or attend these circles of knowledge, such a person is far away from knowledge. Allah describes such a person and says:

وَٱتْلُ عَلَيْهِمْ نَبَأَ ٱلَّذِىٓ ءَاتَيْنَٰهُ ءَايَٰتِنَا فَٱنسَلَخَ مِنْهَا فَأَتْبَعَهُ ٱلشَّيْطَٰنُ فَكَانَ مِنَ ٱلْغَاوِينَ

Relate to them the story of the man to whom We sent our signs, but he passed them by: so Shaitan followed him up, and he went astray. (Quran 7:175)

In other words, Allah is saying 'We made knowledge easily accessible to him, but he passed by, he did not gain the knowledge and became distant from it, so Shaitan found him and took him astray'. Allah continues:

وَلَوْ شِئْنَا لَرَفَعْنَٰهُ بِهَا وَلَٰكِنَّهُۥٓ أَخْلَدَ إِلَى ٱلْأَرْضِ وَٱتَّبَعَ هَوَىٰهُ فَمَثَلُهُۥ كَمَثَلِ ٱلْكَلْبِ إِن تَحْمِلْ عَلَيْهِ يَلْهَثْ أَوْ تَتْرُكْهُ يَلْهَث

If it had been Our will, We should have elevated him with our signs; but he inclined to the Earth, and followed his own vain desires. His similitude is that of a dog: if you attack him, he lolls out his tongue or if you leave him alone, he (still) lolls out his tongue. (Quran 7:176)

In other words, if the person wished to be guided, and Allah intended to guide this person and He accepted this person for guidance, then Allah would elevate this person with knowledge. Knowledge raises a person, but he never took advantage of that knowledge that was easily accessible to him. The knowledge was easily available but he passed it by. This is the meaning of (وَلَٰكِنَّهُۥٓ أَخْلَدَ إِلَى ٱلْأَرْضِ وَٱتَّبَعَ هَوَىٰهُ – but he inclined to the Earth, and followed his own vain desires.).

Allah then describes him and says: (فَمَثَلُهُ كَمَثَلِ ٱلْكَلْبِ إِن تَحْمِلْ عَلَيْهِ يَلْهَثْ أَوْ تَتْرُكْهُ يَلْهَث)

– His similitude is that of a dog: if you attack him, he lolls out his tongue or if you leave him alone, he (still) lolls out his tongue.). Allah gives the illustration of a dog, he lolls his tongue out whether he is standing still or being attacked. The Quran gives a description of the one who puts knowledge aside and ran after the pleasures and the luxuries of this world, he is like a dog who lolls his tongue panting for what he desires, yet he still lolls his tongue when he is not panting [after his desires]. So this is the description of the one who leaves knowledge and becomes busy in this worldly life.

Dear readers, whenever knowledge is accessible to you: whether from scholars, lectures, circles of knowledge, CD's etc. don't walk away from this knowledge and 'loll your tongue' at the desires of this world. In the western environment that we inhabit it is very difficult to find a scholar. So when you do find any one from whom you can benefit, learn from them and increase your knowledge, when such an opportunity arises then grab it with both hands.

A Scene with a Believer Whose Level of Iman is Low

Allah describes a believer whose Iman is not firm and well established in his heart. He is a believer, he believes in Allah and the last and final messenger Prophet Muhammad ﷺ, but he is unsteady in his creed. He is focussed on trying to gain the luxuries of this world, the pleasures of this world, and his desire for this world are greater than his desires for the Hereafter although he is a believer. You will find many people who unfortunately fall into this category. Allah says of such people:

وَمِنَ ٱلنَّاسِ مَن يَعْبُدُ ٱللَّهَ عَلَىٰ حَرْفٍ فَإِنْ أَصَابَهُ خَيْرٌ ٱطْمَأَنَّ بِهِ وَإِنْ أَصَابَتْهُ فِتْنَةٌ ٱنقَلَبَ عَلَىٰ وَجْهِهِ خَسِرَ ٱلدُّنْيَا وَٱلْآخِرَةَ ذَٰلِكَ هُوَ ٱلْخُسْرَانُ ٱلْمُبِينُ

There are among men some who serve Allah, as it were, on the verge: if good befalls them, they are, therewith well content; but if a trial comes to them, they turn away their faces: they lose both this world and the Hereafter: that is loss for all to see! (Quran 22:11)

So there are people who worship Allah on the edge of a mountain, on the edge of the Hell Fire. He worships Allah but at any moment he could fall. Just one step forward and he will fall. He worships Allah, he establishes salah, he gives Zakah but it's all at the edge of the mountain, at the edge of the Hell Fire. If a trial befalls him, he can easily turn away from Allah: as a result he will lose both this world and the Hereafter.

A Scene with one Who Remembers Allah Only in Times of Difficulty

Allah gives another description of the people who are engaged in this world and only remember Allah when a calamity befalls them. For instance, when someone passes away, then they will remember Allah and say: (إنا لله وإنا إليه راجعون -

Surely we belong to Allah and to Him shall we return). They don't establish Salah, they don't remember Allah except in times of difficulty or calamity. Even in times of happiness they don't remember Allah. Let us see how the Quran describes such people;

هُوَ ٱلَّذِى يُسَيِّرُكُمْ فِى ٱلْبَرِّ وَٱلْبَحْرِ حَتَّىٰ إِذَا كُنتُمْ فِى ٱلْفُلْكِ وَجَرَيْنَ بِهِم بِرِيحٍ طَيِّبَةٍ وَفَرِحُواْ بِهَا جَآءَتْهَا رِيحٌ عَاصِفٌ وَجَآءَهُمُ ٱلْمَوْجُ مِن كُلِّ مَكَانٍ وَظَنُّواْ أَنَّهُمْ أُحِيطَ بِهِمْ دَعَوُاْ ٱللَّهَ مُخْلِصِينَ لَهُ ٱلدِّينَ لَئِنْ أَنجَيْتَنَا مِنْ هَٰذِهِ لَنَكُونَنَّ مِنَ ٱلشَّٰكِرِينَ

He is the One who enables you to travel on land and at sea, until when you are aboard the boats, and they sail with those on board, under a favourable wind, and they are pleased with it, there comes upon them a stormy wind, and the wave comes upon them from every direction, and they think that they are surrounded from all sides, they pray to Allah, having faith in Him alone, (and say,) "If You deliver us from this, we shall be grateful indeed." (Quran 10:22)

Allah gives us the image of people sailing in a boat. The weather is beautiful, the Sun is shining, and they are busy enjoying the scene and admiring the beauty. Whilst they are admiring this beauty, a strong wind begins to blow, and waves come at them from all directions. There is sea above, sea below, sea to the right, sea to the left, sea everywhere! They pray to Allah, having faith in Him in times of trouble, and say, "If You save us from this, we shall be grateful indeed." This is how the one who does not remember Allah behaves in times of difficulty. Then what do they do? Allah tells us:

$$\text{فَلَمَّآ أَنجَىٰهُمْ إِذَا هُمْ يَبْغُونَ فِى ٱلْأَرْضِ بِغَيْرِ ٱلْحَقِّ}$$

But when He delivers them, they at once start rebelling on the Earth wrongfully (Quran 10:23)

When Allah saves them then they return to their disobedient ways. This scene illustrates the behaviour of those who only remember Allah in times of difficulty, but when they are happy they transgress.

The Scene of the Battle of the Trench

When we read the Quran, we find Allah has given amazingly descriptive stories therein. The battle of the Trench occurred when non-believers surrounded the Muslims in Madina, and the Jews broke their promise. The hypocrites came to Muhammad ﷺ and said, "O Muhammad, our homes are close to the Jews and they are empty so we fear that our homes will be robbed. Therefore, send us home." Muhammad ﷺ gave them permission to go, and they went to their homes. This reduced the number of Muslims and things became difficult for the Prophet ﷺ and his Companions. Allah describes this scene in the Quran:

$$\text{يَـٰٓأَيُّهَا ٱلَّذِينَ ءَامَنُوا ٱذْكُرُوا نِعْمَةَ ٱللَّهِ عَلَيْكُمْ إِذْ جَآءَتْكُمْ جُنُودٌ فَأَرْسَلْنَا عَلَيْهِمْ رِيحًا وَجُنُودًا لَّمْ}$$
$$\text{تَرَوْهَا وَكَانَ ٱللَّهُ بِمَا تَعْمَلُونَ بَصِيرًا (٩) إِذْ جَآءُوكُم مِّن فَوْقِكُمْ وَمِنْ أَسْفَلَ مِنكُمْ وَإِذْ زَاغَتِ}$$
$$\text{ٱلْأَبْصَـٰرُ وَبَلَغَتِ ٱلْقُلُوبُ ٱلْحَنَاجِرَ وَتَظُنُّونَ بِٱللَّهِ ٱلظُّنُونَا (١٠) هُنَالِكَ ٱبْتُلِىَ ٱلْمُؤْمِنُونَ وَزُلْزِلُوا}$$
$$\text{زِلْزَالًا شَدِيدًا (١١) وَإِذْ يَقُولُ ٱلْمُنَـٰفِقُونَ وَٱلَّذِينَ فِى قُلُوبِهِم مَّرَضٌ مَّا وَعَدَنَا ٱللَّهُ وَرَسُولُهُ إِلَّا}$$
$$\text{غُرُورًا (١٢) وَإِذْ قَالَت طَّآئِفَةٌ مِّنْهُمْ يَـٰٓأَهْلَ يَثْرِبَ لَا مُقَامَ لَكُمْ فَٱرْجِعُوا وَيَسْتَـْٔذِنُ فَرِيقٌ مِّنْهُمُ}$$
$$\text{ٱلنَّبِىَّ يَقُولُونَ إِنَّ بُيُوتَنَا عَوْرَةٌ وَمَا هِىَ بِعَوْرَةٍ إِن يُرِيدُونَ إِلَّا فِرَارًا}$$

O you who believe, remember Allah's favour to you, when the forces (of the infidels) came upon you, and We sent upon them a wind, and the forces (of angels) you did not see. Allah is watchful of whatever you do. Recall, when they came upon you from above you and from below you, and when the eyes were distracted, and the hearts reached the throats, and you were thinking about Allah all sorts of thoughts. At that occasion, the believers were put to a trial they were shaken as by a tremendous shaking. (Remember) when the hypocrites and those having malady in their hearts were saying, "Allah and His messenger did not promise us but deceitfully; And when a group of them said, "O people of Yathrib (Madinah), there is no place for you to stay; so go back." And a group of them was seeking permission (to leave) from the Prophet, saying, "In fact our homes are vulnerable," while they were not vulnerable; they wanted nothing but to escape. (Quran 33:9-13)

These verses have omitted nothing. There is not a single movement, not a single statement, not a single event that Allah has not told us. Allah even tells us the thoughts that the hypocrites had in their hearts. Who can give a better description than Allah? Besides describing to us that which was visible, it also describes to us the invisible, that the hypocrites deceived the Prophet ﷺ by asking for permission to go home in fear that their houses may be robbed. Glory be to Allah who sent down the Quran, and gave this most accurate description of the battle.

The Scene of the Battle of Uhud

Let's look at a description of another battle, the battle of Uhud. At the start of this battle the Muslims were expected to be victorious, as Allah said:

$$وَلَقَدْ صَدَقَكُمُ ٱللَّهُ وَعْدَهُ إِذْ تَحُسُّونَهُم بِإِذْنِهِ$$

Allah has surely fulfilled His promise to you when you, with His will, were killing them off. (Quran 3:152)

Then Allah describes to us what happened during the battle. The Muslims were defeated because they made a big mistake. Allah says:

$$حَتَّىٰٓ إِذَا فَشِلْتُمْ وَتَنَٰزَعْتُمْ فِى ٱلْأَمْرِ وَعَصَيْتُم مِّنۢ بَعْدِ مَآ أَرَىٰكُم مَّا تُحِبُّونَ مِنكُم مَّن يُرِيدُ ٱلدُّنْيَا$$
$$وَمِنكُم مَّن يُرِيدُ ٱلْأَخِرَةَ$$

Until you showed weakness and disputed in the matter and disobeyed after He had shown you what you liked. Among you there were some who were seeking the world, and among you there were others who were seeking the Hereafter. (Quran 3:152)

A companion of the Prophet ﷺ upon hearing this verse, said, 'By Allah, we didn't know that there were amongst us those whose intention was for this world.' The Quran describes their intentions. The books of seerah do not tell us about their intentions, but the Quran does. The description by Allah in the Quran tells us both their outer state and their inner state (innermost thoughts and desires).

Suppose a calamity befalls a person, he comes and tells you of his calamity, and then says, "You don't understand what I am going through". This is true, because you cannot understand what that person is going through. But the One Who is giving this description of their hearts and their inner state is One Who is fully aware of people's thoughts and hearts. Allah further says:

$$\text{يَظُنُّونَ بِٱللَّهِ غَيْرَ ٱلْحَقِّ ظَنَّ ٱلْجَٰهِلِيَّةِ}$$

They thought of Allah unjustly, the thought[s] [born] of ignorance. (Quran 3:154)

This is referring to the hypocrites when they thought that the disbelievers had achieved ultimate victory and that Islam and its people would perish. So Allah, besides describing the battle to us, He also describes their invisible and private intentions. The Prophet ﷺ did not know what was in their hearts, but Allah describes to us what they said to themselves. How extraordinary it is that the Quran allows us such detailed access to the invisible truths of this event.

Dear readers, next time you read the Quran, my advice is that you get into the habit of pausing upon every verse and reflecting upon the descriptions detailed in the verses. There are many verses on every page in which Allah describes various scenes for us. And pondering and reflecting upon them will increase your obedience to Allah.

The Scene of the Day of Resurrection

Allah provides us with a vivid glimpse of the Day of Resurrection; the day which every one of us is destined to face in the next life:

وَلَا تَحْسَبَنَّ ٱللَّهَ غَٰفِلًا عَمَّا يَعْمَلُ ٱلظَّٰلِمُونَ إِنَّمَا يُؤَخِّرُهُمْ لِيَوْمٍ تَشْخَصُ فِيهِ ٱلْأَبْصَٰرُ

(٤٢) مُهْطِعِينَ مُقْنِعِى رُءُوسِهِمْ لَا يَرْتَدُّ إِلَيْهِمْ طَرْفُهُمْ وَأَفْـِٔدَتُهُمْ هَوَآءٌ

Never think that Allah is unaware of what the wrongdoers are doing. He is but giving them respite up to a day when the eyes shall remain upraised (in terror). (42) They shall be rushing with their heads raised upward; their eyes shall not return towards them and their hearts shall be hollow. (Quran 14:42-43)

A frightening, scary, terrifying description of what the Day of Resurrection has in store for the unbelievers, achieved in just a few words of the Quran.

There are many descriptions of this day to be found in the Quran, but I will mention only one more, where Allah talks about the arguments that will take place amongst the non-believers on their way to the Fire:

هَٰذَا فَوْجٌ مُّقْتَحِمٌ مَّعَكُمْ لَا مَرْحَبًۢا بِهِمْ إِنَّهُمْ صَالُوا۟ ٱلنَّارِ (٥٩) قَالُوا۟ بَلْ أَنتُمْ لَا مَرْحَبًۢا بِكُمْ

أَنتُمْ قَدَّمْتُمُوهُ لَنَا فَبِئْسَ ٱلْقَرَارُ (٦٠) قَالُوا۟ رَبَّنَا مَن قَدَّمَ لَنَا هَٰذَا فَزِدْهُ عَذَابًا ضِعْفًا فِى ٱلنَّارِ

(٦١) وَقَالُوا۟ مَا لَنَا لَا نَرَىٰ رِجَالًا كُنَّا نَعُدُّهُم مِّنَ ٱلْأَشْرَارِ (٦٢) أَتَّخَذْنَٰهُمْ سِخْرِيًّا أَمْ زَاغَتْ

عَنْهُمُ ٱلْأَبْصَٰرُ (٦٣) إِنَّ ذَٰلِكَ لَحَقٌّ تَخَاصُمُ أَهْلِ ٱلنَّارِ

This is a crowd rushing in along with you; no welcome for them; verily they are to roast in the Fire. They will say nay! It is you, for whom there is no welcome: it is you who have brought it upon us. Evil shall be the resting-place. They Will say: Our Lord! Whosoever hath brought this upon us, – Unto him increase doubly the torment of the Fire. And they will say: "What has happened to us that we see not men whom we used to number among the bad ones? Had we taken them as a laughing-stock (unjustly), or have our eyes missed them?" That is going to happen definitely, that is, the mutual quarrel of the people of the Fire. (Quran 38:59-64)

This tells us that there will be quarrels between those on their way to the Hell Fire. They will say, 'It is not for me, but for you'; 'Where are those we called sinners? Are they not here?' People will have judged others not knowing that they themselves are among the sinners, and so condemned to the Hell Fire. This was in brief the description of the Day of Judgement and the conversation that will take place in the Hell amongst the non-believers.

Ibn Masood ﷺ said: "Don't read the Quran like a story book. Instead pause at every magnificent verse of the Quran, and shake your hearts."

ءَامِنُواْ بِهِۦٓ أَوۡ لَا تُؤۡمِنُوٓاْ إِنَّ ٱلَّذِينَ أُوتُواْ ٱلۡعِلۡمَ مِن قَبۡلِهِۦٓ إِذَا يُتۡلَىٰ عَلَيۡهِمۡ يَخِرُّونَ لِلۡأَذۡقَانِ سُجَّدًا (١٠٧) وَيَقُولُونَ سُبۡحَٰنَ رَبِّنَآ إِن كَانَ وَعۡدُ رَبِّنَا لَمَفۡعُولاً (١٠٨) وَيَخِرُّونَ لِلۡأَذۡقَانِ يَبۡكُونَ وَيَزِيدُهُمۡ خُشُوعًا

Whether ye believe in it or not, it is true that those who were given knowledge beforehand, when it is recited to them, fall down on their faces in humble prostration And say: "Glory to our Lord! Truly has the promise of our Lord been fulfilled!" They fall down on their faces in tears, and it increases their (earnest) humility. (Quran 17:107-109)

Summary

Today, you have learnt some of the miracles within the Quran, specifically the scenes described for us. Allah describes scenes for us because a picture painted in front of us makes things much clearer. That is why, on every page of the Quran, Allah paints such vivid pictures for us. It is another miracle of the Quran.

Many of us are unaware of these miracles, but discovering them will only increase your love for the Quran. The more you love this book, the more you will want to learn, and the more you will want to spend quality time with the Quran.

Workshop

The quiz questions and the exercises are provided to further your understanding. Don't worry if you can't answer all of the questions in the quiz. Try your best to answer as many as you can. You are recommended to go through the chapter to check your answers to these questions.

Quiz 5

1. How does Allah describe those who reject His signs?
2. How does Allah describe the deeds of the non-believers?

3. How does Allah describe a person who does not take advantage of accessible knowledge?

2

- Scientific Miracles in the Universe and on the Earth mentioned in the Quran
- Scientific Miracles of the Human Body mentioned in the Quran
- Other Miracles; Miracle of Numbers, Environment, Laws, Logic

Scientific Miracles in the Universe Mentioned in the Quran

DAY 6

Introduction to the Scientific Miracles

The main purpose of sharing these miracles is to connect readers to the Quran. Without understanding the Quran, recitation is only 'recitation without a spirit' like Ibn Masood's ﷺ statement mentioned in the previous chapter. A person's aim is not to simply finish reading the Quran once, twice, or hundreds of times. My purpose in describing these miracles is to connect you with the book of Allah, so that when you recite, you understand, you taste the sweetness, and realize that there is a miracle right in front of you. The more attached you are to the book of Allah, the more your Iman will increase, and the more your Iman increases the more you will get closer in your relationship with Allah.

The problem with people not following Islam nowadays is not that they don't have knowledge. Most of us know what is right and wrong; we have knowledge. The problem is that people have not reached the level of Iman at which they would make positive changes in their lives. When they see these miracles then the inclination to follow the commands of Allah increases. A believer does not normally require someone to come and warn him or scare him or frighten him. What he requires is for someone to come and talk to him about the greatness of Allah. Once he has reached the level of Iman by knowing Who Allah is, he will realize that Allah has power over all things and his Iman will increase. As a result it will become easy for him to follow the commands of Allah. So in sharing these miracles the aim is to help you increase your Iman. It is not that we are not believers. We are believers, Alhumdulillah! Many people have Iman but they don't follow the commands of Allah. When they study these miracles their Iman will increase, and whoever's Iman increases, they will have no choice but to follow Allah's commands.

قُلْ إِن كُنتُمْ تُحِبُّونَ ٱللَّهَ فَٱتَّبِعُونِي يُحْبِبْكُمُ ٱللَّهُ

Say: "If ye do love Allah, follow me: Allah will love you" (Quran 3:31)

In this chapter we will be discussing the scientific miracles in the Quran. Scholars say that there are approximately 900 verses in the Quran that talk about science. Today's lesson is dedicated to studying the miracles in the universe mentioned in the Quran. Allah says:

سَنُرِيهِمْ ءَايٰتِنَا فِى ٱلْأَفَاقِ

Soon will We show them Our Signs in the (furthest) regions (of the Earth) (Quran 41:53).

Allah begins this verse with the letter (س) which denotes the future. Many things were not clear at the time of Prophet Muhammad ﷺ, but since science has advanced, things have started to become clearer and therefore visible to us. In the past 30 – 40 years the quantity of scientific knowledge has advanced astonishingly. In terms of knowledge available, in the last 40 years mankind has discovered so much that the "new" is equal to what people learned from the time of creation and the beginning of man. Our knowledge has doubled in 40 years. How astonishing! The Quran mentions certain things which were impossible to understand previous to the "recent" discoveries of science. We have not reached the end of science – we do not know everything – neither have we reached the end of the commentary of the Quran; and the treasures of the Quran are inexhaustible. So the verse begins with (س) which indicates the future continuous tense. In another place Allah says:

سَأُوْرِيكُمْ ءَايٰتِى فَلَا تَسْتَعْجِلُونِ

Soon (enough) will I show you My Signs: then ye will not ask Me to hasten them! (Quran 21:37)

In other words: 'We have not shown you some signs, O Muhammad, I will show them later.' Many of these scientific miracles were not known or understood at the time of Muhammad ﷺ, but we know about them today.

There are many of these scientific miracles in the Quran. We will divide them into two main categories: signs in the universe and signs in the human body. Allah says:

$$وَفِي أَنفُسِكُمْ أَفَلَا تُبْصِرُونَ$$

As also in your own selves: will ye not then see? (Quran 51:21)

Allah commands you to look for, and see, these signs in the universe and within yourself. Allah wants you to search for these signs. When you gaze at these signs with your heart, your heart will be filled with light. Allah says:

$$قَدْ جَآءَكُم بَصَآئِرُ مِن رَّبِّكُمْ فَمَنْ أَبْصَرَ فَلِنَفْسِهِ$$

Now have come to you from your Lord, proofs (to open your eyes): if any will see, it, will be for (the good of) his own soul; (Quran 6:104)

$$إِنَّ فِي ذَٰلِكَ لَآيَٰتٍ لِّقَوْمٍ يَتَفَكَّرُونَ$$

Verily in that are Signs for those who reflect. (Quran 30:21)

These signs are not for everyone, they are for those who reflect and ponder and look at and examine the signs of Allah. You see the signs with your eyes but you probably don't reflect on them? Allah says:

$$ٱلَّذِينَ يَذْكُرُونَ ٱللَّهَ قِيَٰمًا وَقُعُودًا وَعَلَىٰ جُنُوبِهِمْ وَيَتَفَكَّرُونَ فِي خَلْقِ ٱلسَّمَٰوَٰتِ وَٱلْأَرْضِ رَبَّنَا$$

$$مَا خَلَقْتَ هَٰذَا بَٰطِلًا سُبْحَٰنَكَ فَقِنَا عَذَابَ ٱلنَّارِ$$

[Those] Who remember Allah standing and sitting, and (lying) on their sides, and ponder on the creation of the Heavens and the Earth (and say) "Our Lord, You have not created all this in vain. We proclaim Your purity. So, save us from the punishment of Fire. (Quran 3:191)

If Allah was talking about reflecting on those of His signs that we are able to see with our eyes, like the Sun, the Moon, the mountains etc, Allah would not have said

(سَنُرِيهِمْ — Soon we will show them) because the Companions and the Prophet ﷺ were already looking at these signs:

$$أَفَلَا يَنظُرُونَ إِلَى ٱلْإِبِلِ كَيْفَ خُلِقَتْ (١٧) وَإِلَى ٱلسَّمَآءِ كَيْفَ رُفِعَتْ (١٨) وَإِلَى ٱلْجِبَالِ كَيْفَ نُصِبَتْ (١٩) وَإِلَى ٱلْأَرْضِ كَيْفَ سُطِحَتْ$$

So, do they not look at the camels how they are created, (17) And at the sky, how it is raised high, (18) And at the mountains, how they are

installed, (19) And at the Earth, how it is spread out? (Quran 88:17-20)

Here Allah is talking about seeing the signs in the mountains and in the camels, in things which the people at that time were able to see. They were not able to see the universe, due to lack of technologies, but Allah knew that in the future mankind would be able to see the universe. This is why Allah said 'We will soon show them our signs.' Allah further says:

$$وَقُلِ ٱلْحَمْدُ لِلَّهِ سَيُرِيكُمْ ءَايَٰتِهِ فَتَعْرِفُونَهَا$$

Say, "Praise belongs to Allah. He will show you His signs, then you will recognize them." (Quran 27:93)

Allah is saying 'He will [at a future time] show you His signs,' meaning, not in the lifetime of Muhammad ﷺ. In fact, in every era He will show you His signs. When you see a sign you will recognize it and say, 'Oh, the Quran mentions and talks about this sign', and you will recognize these signs.

So, the signs that are close to us and that we can see with our naked eyes are very clear. As for those signs that lie out in the universe and those that exist within us, we must realize that Allah does not want us to look at them with the naked eye, He wants us to look beyond what the eye can see.

The Invention of Telescopes

Seeing the universe requires equipment to help the naked eye to see further. Similarly, seeing inside ourselves requires equipment to help the naked eye. We were not able to achieve these things until the invention of lenses and therefore telescopes and microscopes. The telescope was invented in the year 1609. That is approximately 1000 years after the Prophet's time ﷺ. So, people were unaware of many of these visionary verses in the Quran for about 1000 years. These signs were not known to humans *as signs* until the invention of telescopes. The basic telescope was invented in the year 1609, but it was very low powered. As the science of lens making advanced, they strengthened telescope power to 1000x, [strength] then it reached 2000x [strength]. Even so, the real discoveries in the universe did not start until the invention of the radio telescope, which was invented in the year 1937.

First Telescope built by Galileo Galilei in 1609

First Radio Telescope built by Grote Reber in 1937

The evolution of the radio telescope has increased 'the visible universe' tremendously. The optical telescope took us from doubling the magnification (2x) to over 2000x. Today, the radio telescopes have raised the magnification to a million times (perhaps even more) more than the naked eye. And in the last decade new telescopes (which may cost 1000 million dollars or more), which, even in poor visibility due to clouds, and the pollution of artificial lighting show us even more of space. Scientists are constantly making discoveries that we were not able to see before.

Important Points When Examining Science in the Quran

These technologies have opened up new doors, and so we can increase our knowledge about the scientific signs mentioned in the Quran. But before we look into these verses I would like to make few points clear:

Firstly, although the Quran contains over 900 verses that speaks of science, nevertheless the Quran is not a book of science, it is a book of guidance. Allah says in the Quran:

هُدًى لِّلنَّاسِ

Guidance for mankind (Quran 2:185)

So, the Quran is *not* a book of science, but it *is* a book of guidance.

Secondly, the Quran talks about many different topics. It does not only talk about one specific topic throughout the book. The Quran talks about Science, Biology, Chemistry, Physics, History, Logic etc. So whatever topic interests you, the Quran will talk about it. If you are interested in poetry, the Quran talks about poetry. If you are interested in science and technology, the Quran talks about science and technology. Whichever field you are interested in, the Quran contains insights pertaining to that field, and it will quench your thirst for knowledge. That is why Allah says:

وَلَقَدْ صَرَّفْنَا فِى هَٰذَا ٱلْقُرْءَانِ لِلنَّاسِ مِن كُلِّ مَثَلٍ وَكَانَ ٱلْإِنسَٰنُ أَكْثَرَ شَىْءٍ جَدَلًا

We have explained in detail in this Quran, for the benefit of mankind, every kind of similitude: but man is, in most things contentious. (Quran 18:54)

Thirdly, some people go to the extreme. They say that there is nothing in the Quran that talks about science. This is an extreme view and it is not true. The Quran makes many observations that impinge on scientific knowledge, but we need to be aware of some of the conditions mentioned below before talking about any scientific points. We do not go to extremes, we do not deny the meaning of any verse in the Quran and neither do we say that there are no verses in the Quran that have scientific implications; there has to be a balance between the two. But when discussing science, pay attention to the following important points:

a) The Quran's special brand of eloquence means that it contains many layers of meaning. The earlier scholars may have derived certain meanings, with which we may not necessarily disagree, but today, due to advancements in science and technology we may sometimes find interpretations that are more accurate and precise, that earlier scholars could not have arrived at due to the relative lack of technical resources.

b) Some people go to another extreme, and they say that nothing about science is factual; that it is only theory. Again, this is not true, because if a scientific point has become a fact and it does not contradict the Quran then we should believe in it. For example, the shape of the Earth is spherical, you cannot argue with this scientific fact. You can't have doubts about established scientific facts. It is impossible that the world is any shape other than spherical, because Allah has given us intelligence, and He has shown us proofs in the Quran and signs in the universe. He has given us the technology to enable us to look for these truths, and when such scientific findings do not contradict the Quran, then there is no need to have doubts about these facts. In fact, when the Quran confirms these scientific facts, this should strengthen our Iman.

c) It is impossible to find a contradiction between real scientific facts and the Quran. It is not possible that an established scientific fact contradicts the Quran, because the One who created the universe sent down the Quran. So, if we believe that Allah has created the universe and that He is the One Who has revealed the Quran, then there will never be a genuine contradiction between the two.

d) Using logic and science to understand the Quran is not something new, it was happening at the time of the Companions of the Prophet ﷺ. The Quran stresses the importance for people to think, to reason and to use their mind and intellect. The word "mind" or "reasoning" is mentioned 49 times in the Quran to emphasize on the importance for people to think.

Scientific Miracles in the Heavens and the Universe

We will start with the scientific miracles in the Heavens and the Universe that are mentioned in the Quran. Many people think that we human beings are the greatest creation of Allah. But Allah tells us:

لَخَلْقُ ٱلسَّمَٰوَٰتِ وَٱلْأَرْضِ أَكْبَرُ مِنْ خَلْقِ ٱلنَّاسِ وَلَٰكِنَّ أَكْثَرَ ٱلنَّاسِ لَا يَعْلَمُونَ

Certainly, the creation of the Heavens and the Earth is greater than the

creation of human beings, but most human beings do not know. (Quran 40:57)

We human beings are not the greatest creation, it is the creation of the Heavens and the Earth which is greater than the creation of human beings. This is why Allah tells us in the Quran to look at the Heavens, because when we look at the creation that is greater than us humans, our Iman and Faith with Allah increases. Allah says:

ٱلَّذِى خَلَقَ سَبْعَ سَمَٰوَٰتٍ طِبَاقًا مَّا تَرَىٰ فِى خَلْقِ ٱلرَّحْمَٰنِ مِن تَفَٰوُتٍ فَٱرْجِعِ ٱلْبَصَرَ هَلْ تَرَىٰ مِن فُطُورٍ (٣) ثُمَّ ٱرْجِعِ ٱلْبَصَرَ كَرَّتَيْنِ يَنقَلِبْ إِلَيْكَ ٱلْبَصَرُ خَاسِئًا وَهُوَ حَسِيرٌ

[He] Who has created seven skies, one over the other. You will see nothing out of proportion in the creation of the Rahman (Allah the All-Merciful). So, cast your eye again. Do you see any rifts? Then cast your eye again and again, and your sight will return to you in a state of humiliation and worn out. (Quran 67:3-4)

6

Allah is telling us to examine the Heavens closely and repeatedly, and He further stresses the point because we cannot gather all of the minute details and signs in the universe in a single attempt. So, we must look again and again.

Looking at the Universe is an Act of Worship

Many people limit religion to just praying, fasting and other rituals, but Allah commands us to observe the universe, He wants us to turn our sight to the Heavens, and in doing so, our Iman increases, which will bring us closer to Allah. Allah says:

أَوَلَمْ يَنظُرُوا۟ فِى مَلَكُوتِ ٱلسَّمَٰوَٰتِ وَٱلْأَرْضِ وَمَا خَلَقَ ٱللَّهُ مِن شَىْءٍ

Have they not looked into the kingdom of the Heavens and the Earth, and into the things Allah has created? (Quran 7:185)

In another verse Allah says:

قُلِ ٱنظُرُوا۟ مَاذَا فِى ٱلسَّمَٰوَٰتِ وَٱلْأَرْضِ

Say, "Look at what is there in the Heavens and the Earth." (Quran 10:101)

These verses are a command given by Allah, which makes looking in the Heavens and the Earth an act of worship and obedience to Allah, not just a pastime. So, we should follow this command of Allah to look at the universe. Allah condemns those who do not look at the universe. Allah says:

أَفَلَمْ يَنظُرُوٓا۟ إِلَى ٱلسَّمَآءِ فَوْقَهُمْ كَيْفَ بَنَيْنَٰهَا وَزَيَّنَّٰهَا وَمَا لَهَا مِن فُرُوجٍ

Did they not, then, look to the sky above them, how We have built it and beautified it, and it has no cracks? (Quran 50:6)

Creation of the Heavens with Invisible Pillars

The universe is an amazing topic. We will now look at some of the verses in the Quran that talk about the creation of the universe. Allah talks about the creation of the Heavens; Allah says:

خَلَقَ ٱلسَّمَٰوَٰتِ بِغَيْرِ عَمَدٍ تَرَوْنَهَا

He created the Heavens without any pillars that ye can see (Quran 31:10)

Some commentators of the Quran say that this verse means that the Heavens are without pillars. Others say that the Heavens do have pillars, but you cannot see them. The correct opinion is of those scholars who say that Heavens do have pillars, because if they didn't, Allah would have said: (خَلَقَ ٱلسَّمَٰوَٰتِ بِغَيْرِ عَمَدٍ – He created the Heavens without any pillars), then it would mean the Heavens do not have pillars. But Allah didn't say that, He said: (خَلَقَ ٱلسَّمَٰوَٰتِ بِغَيْرِ عَمَدٍ تَرَوْنَهَا – He created the Heavens without any pillars that ye can see) meaning (تَرَوْنَ الْعَمَد – You see the pillars) Allah is not saying 'you cannot see the Heavens' because the possessive adjective (هَا) attaches to the closest noun in that sentence, in which case it is 'pillars' and not 'the Heavens'. We are not saying that the other commentators are wrong, we are saying that the second meaning (that the Heavens have pillars) is more authentic and closer to the meaning of the Quran and the Hadith. So now the question may arise, where are these pillars that the Quran is referring to?

Before we understand where these pillars are, let me clarify the meaning of (سَمَاء – Heavens). (سَمَاء – Heavens) is everything above you, it is not just the Heavens. Everything above you is called (سَمَاء). So (سَمَاء) includes everything in creation that is above you, including the stars, the Sun, the Moon, the planets, the entire solar system, and every creation of Allah that is above you. So, who controls this creation? Who controls the Sun? The Moon? The Stars? So that they don't fall on you and so that they don't collide with each other? Scientists say that this 'pillar' is gravity. If there were no gravity, then the skies and Heavens would collapse and fall

down into utter ruin. The universe would collapse. The Sun and the Moon would collide with each other. This will all happen on the Day of Judgement. So the existence of gravity protects the universe from collapsing. It is gravity, that holds everything in its place or else the entire universe would collapse. Praise be to Allah who created this gravity.

What is One Day Equal to?

In the Quran Allah talks about one day being equal to 1000 years and in another verse Allah talks about one day being equal to 50,000 years. Let us examine both verses. Allah says:

وَإِنَّ يَوْمًا عِندَ رَبِّكَ كَأَلْفِ سَنَةٍ مِّمَّا تَعُدُّونَ

Verily, one day with your Lord is like one thousand years according to your calculation (Quran 22:47)

In another verse Allah says:

تَعْرُجُ ٱلْمَلَٰٓئِكَةُ وَٱلرُّوحُ إِلَيْهِ فِى يَوْمٍ كَانَ مِقْدَارُهُ خَمْسِينَ أَلْفَ سَنَةٍ

The angels and the Spirit ascend unto Him in a Day the measure whereof is (as) fifty thousand years (Quran 70:4)

In the first verse Allah says that the day is equal to 1000 years, in the second verse Allah says that the day is equal to 50,000 years. Which is correct? Let's look at this topic, which, according to the scientists, is the topic of 'the relativity of time'. We know there are 24 hours in a day, of course, and 365 days make a year. But if you look at Venus, you will find that 1 day on Venus is equal to 8 months on Earth. And 1 year on Venus is equal to 7 months on Earth. (Yes, Venus's day is longer than it's year) Let's look at Mercury, 1 year on Mercury is equal to 88 Earth days. So I ask you now, is 1 year equal to 88 days or is 1 year equal to 7 months? The answer is the relativity of time. When you look at Science and the Universe, you will find that these variations depend upon the relativity of time. So when Allah talks about the day, and in one verse He says that it is equal to 1000 years and in another verse He says it is equal to 50,000 years, they are both correct because there is relativity of time.

Things in the Universe that we Know of and Things we Don't Know of

Allah says in the Quran:

فَلَآ أُقْسِمُ بِمَا تُبْصِرُونَ (٣٨) وَمَا لَا تُبْصِرُونَ

I swear by what you see (38) And what you do not see (Quran 69:38-39)

There are so many things in the universe that we know and yet much more that we still don't know. Allah says:

وَمَآ أُوتِيتُم مِّنَ ٱلْعِلْمِ إِلَّا قَلِيلاً

And you are not given from the knowledge but a little. (Quran 17:85)

But there is another thing that I find more amazing. When the sky is dark, and you look up at it, you can see lots of stars. On an average night you will be able to see around 2000 stars. On a very dark night, when the darkness is intense, you may be able to see 3000 – 4000 stars. The absolute maximum you can see is up to 5000 stars.

Science tells us that the Milky Way, the galaxy which encompasses us, which contains our solar system, is composed of an estimated 300 – 500 thousand million stars. We cannot see them, even in the clearest night. The maximum we can see is up to 5000 stars. Allah says: I swear by that which ye see. And that which ye see not. (Quran 69:38-39)

The Creation of the Universe

In the 1970's a group of scientists described the creation of the universe and they called it the 'Big Bag'. Allah gives the description of the creation of the Universe and says:

أَوَلَمْ يَرَ ٱلَّذِينَ كَفَرُوٓاْ أَنَّ ٱلسَّمَٰوَٰتِ وَٱلْأَرْضَ كَانَتَا رَتْقًا فَفَتَقْنَٰهُمَا

Do not the unbelievers see that the Heavens and the Earth were joined together (as one unit of Creation), before We clove them aSunder? (Quran 21:30)

(رَتْق) means joined together, combined together. Meaning that the Heavens were joined with Earth and then He tore them asunder. The amazing thing here is that the earlier scholars, commentators on the Quran, also said the same thing about the Heavens and the Earth even though the Big Bang theory was only recently proposed.

Ibn Abbas ﷺ says that the Heavens and the Earth were both joined together 'so Allah raised the Heavens and laid down the Earth'. Hassan and Qatadah عليهما رحمة الله made similar statements. So the Quran is very clear, and the commentary on the Quran is also clear, that the Heavens and the Earth were joined together and Allah wrenched them apart. Scientists described this unity of the Heavens and the Earth, but the Quran's description of it is more marvellous. Allah says:

ثُمَّ ٱسْتَوَىٰ إِلَى ٱلسَّمَآءِ وَهِىَ دُخَانٌ

Then He turned straight to the sky, while it was a smoke (Quran 41:11)

Allah is saying that the Heavens were formed of smoke and gas. All of these minute details that the Quran describes have been confirmed by science.

Let us look at how this universe came into existence. Everything in the universe, in the cosmos, all of space, was in a form smaller than a subatomic particle. For many years the only subatomic particles known were Protons, Neutrons and Electrons. As technology advanced, scientists found that there are smaller particles. Protons and Neutrons are a similar size and Electrons are much smaller. Now scientists study yet smaller particles, the Quark, (and smaller yet) the Gluon.

The question is, what exploded this universe in the event which we today call the Big Bang? What was the cause of this expansion? When we consider that the entire universe was smaller than a particle, and from this particle the entire universe, the

Earth, the Stars, the Sun, the Moon etc. came into existence; the question is, what caused this amazing phenomenon? Scientists do not know as yet what caused this expansion of the universe, but we Muslims say it was the command of Allah and the two letters that caused this expansion. It was the letters (كُنْ – Be) and it was done.

If you reflect for a moment on the above mentioned verse, (أَوَلَمْ يَرَ ٱلَّذِينَ كَفَرُوٓاْ أَنَّ ٱلسَّمَٰوَٰتِ وَٱلْأَرْضَ), Allah didn't use the singular form for Heaven, Allah didn't say (سَّمَاء) Allah used the plural form and said (سَمَٰوَٰتِ) meaning that everything that was above you was joined together with the Earth. Then it was wrenched asunder by the power of Allah, and began shaping itself over time.

Description of the Moon in the Quran

Allah says:

$$\text{وَٱلْقَمَرَ قَدَّرْنَٰهُ مَنَازِلَ حَتَّىٰ عَادَ كَٱلْعُرْجُونِ ٱلْقَدِيمِ}$$

And the Moon— We have measured for it mansions (to traverse) till it returns like the old (and withered) lower part of a date-stalk. (Quran 36:39)

Allah describes the moon as (عُرْجُونٍ) and (عُرْجُونٍ) is a branch of the palm tree, if you take off the leaves you will be left with a branch. There are two things that would happen to this branch as it gets older. Firstly, the branch curves, and secondly, it gets thinner. This is exactly the description of the Moon. Once the Moon is full it then starts to thin and curve, thin and curve, thin and curve, until it becomes like an old palm tree branch.

Description of the Moon given in the Quran

The Speed of the Earth

A spot on the surface of the Earth is moving at 1675 Kilometres/hour or 465 metres/second. That's 1040 Miles/hour, 1675 Kilometres/hour. Imagine, every second you are moving almost half a kilometre in space and you don't even feel it! The Earth revolves around the Sun. The Sun pulls the Earth (due to gravity) and the Earth rotates with the Sun, the Moon, and all the Planets at an amazingly fast speed.

The Expanding Universe

Allah says in the Quran:

وَٱلسَّمَآءَ بَنَيْنَٰهَا بِأَيْيْدٍ وَإِنَّا لَمُوسِعُونَ

And the sky was built by Us with might; and indeed We are the expanders.
(Quran 51:47)

Scholars say that the Earth is not expand*ed*, it is expand*ing*. Albert Einstein theorised that the Earth was no longer expanding, and held this belief until 1931. In April of that year he adopted the model of an expanding universe, and now it is an accepted scientific fact that the universe is expanding.

Allah, the Knower of the Visible and the Unseen

Allah says in the Quran:

عَـٰلِمُ ٱلْغَيْبِ وَٱلشَّهَـٰدَةِ

All-Knower of the Unseen and the seen, (Quran 32:6)

When Allah says that He is the Knower of the Unseen, we are not surprised because of course Allah is the knower of the Unseen. But Allah praises Himself, saying that He is also the Knower of the Seen. What does this mean? Aren't we too the knowers of the Seen; we too can see the Sun, the Moon, the Stars and so forth. Why is Allah praising Himself and telling us that He is the Knower of the Seen?

Everything that we see in this world or in this universe is a snapshot of a past event, it is not as it appears now. Light travels very fast but it still takes time to travel from one place to another. So when you see something in this world or in the universe, what you are actually doing is using your eyes to detect the light that is reflected by an object. So, suppose you look at a clock, you are not seeing the clock as it is now, but as it was a tiny fraction of a second ago. Since light travels so fast it doesn't really make a difference over such a short distance, and it is difficult to tell the difference. It makes a big difference though, when you start to look at the universe.

If you look at the Moon, think how far the light that is reflecting has to travel before it hits your eyes. The Moon is a lot further away than a clock so it takes a bit more than a second to get to you. That means that when you see the Moon, you are not seeing it as it is now but as it was a second ago. The Sun is much further away than the Moon so *that* light takes approximately eight minutes to reach you. In other words, when you look at the Sun you are not seeing the Sun as it is now, but as it was eight minutes ago. The light from other Stars takes years. Light from the nearest Star, Proxima Centauri, takes 4.23 years to reach us. So when you look at anything in space you are seeing a snapshot of the past. Back to that question now, are you the Knower of the Seen? No, you are not because you are seeing the snapshot of a previous event. This is why Allah praises Himself, saying that He is the Knower of all things Unseen and the Seen.

The End of the Universe

Scientists have agreed that the universe is expanding. There is, however, another theory that calls the end of this universe 'The Big Crunch'. This theory says that there will be a huge destruction and the universe will collapse. The Stars will fall, the Sun and the Moon will be destroyed. This theory gives one possible description of how this universe will end. This is very similar to the description given to us by Allah in the Quran. Allah says:

يَسْـَٔلُ أَيَّانَ يَوْمُ ٱلْقِيَٰمَةِ (٦) فَإِذَا بَرِقَ ٱلْبَصَرُ (٧) وَخَسَفَ ٱلْقَمَرُ (٨) وَجُمِعَ ٱلشَّمْسُ وَٱلْقَمَرُ (٩) يَقُولُ ٱلْإِنسَٰنُ يَوْمَئِذٍ أَيْنَ ٱلْمَفَرُّ

He asks, "When will be this Day of Resurrection?" So, when the eyes will be dazzled, And the Moon will lose its light, And the Sun and the Moon will be joined together, On that day man will say, "Where to escape?" (Quran 75:6-10)

So the theory of 'The Big Crunch' is similar to the description of the end of the universe given in these verses. Although that theory still remains only a theory, for us Muslims – because Allah revealed the Quran and He has informed us that this is how the universe will end – therefore, for us Muslims, this is a fact.

The Black Hole

There is another theory of how this universe will come to an end. There is a Black Hole located in the centre of the Earth's galaxy, in the middle of the Milky Way and the Earth orbits this Black Hole. The scientists have noticed that as the Earth orbits this Black Hole, it gets closer to the Black Hole. The effect of the Black Hole is such that whatever falls into it, is "stretched like spaghetti" by the gravitational gradient from head to toe. This too is a theory but the Quran tells us:

كُلُّ مَنْ عَلَيْهَا فَانٍ

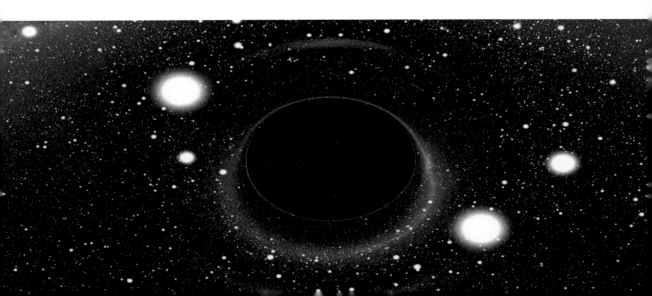

All that is on Earth will perish; (Quran 55:26)

According to science these are all theories, but all their theories show us that this universe is not permanent and eventually will come to an end.

Summary

Today you have learnt some of the scientific miracles in the universe mentioned in the Quran. These miracles are signs from Allah, and the purpose of every sign is to direct you to a destination. When you drive your car and you see road signs, London is 50 miles, Paris is 30 miles and so on – what is the purpose of these signs? They are directing you to your destination. Similarly, the purpose of every sign given by Allah is to direct you back to Him. If these signs do not direct you to Allah then it defeats the purpose of the sign. So, whenever you look at the signs of Allah, declare the greatness of Allah, increase your Iman, and take yourself back to Allah.

إِنَّ فِى خَلْقِ ٱلسَّمَٰوَٰتِ وَٱلْأَرْضِ وَٱخْتِلَٰفِ ٱلَّيْلِ وَٱلنَّهَارِ لَأَيَٰتٍ لِّأُوْلِى ٱلْأَلْبَٰبِ (١٩٠) ٱلَّذِينَ يَذْكُرُونَ ٱللَّهَ قِيَٰمًا وَقُعُودًا وَعَلَىٰ جُنُوبِهِمْ وَيَتَفَكَّرُونَ فِى خَلْقِ ٱلسَّمَٰوَٰتِ وَٱلْأَرْضِ رَبَّنَا مَا خَلَقْتَ هَٰذَا بَٰطِلاً سُبْحَٰنَكَ فَقِنَا عَذَابَ ٱلنَّارِ

Surely, in the creation of the Heavens and the Earth, and in the alternation of night and day, there are signs for the people of wisdom, Who remember Allah standing and sitting, and (lying) on their sides, and ponder on the creation of the Heavens and the Earth (and say) "Our Lord, You have not created all this in vain. We proclaim Your purity. So, save us from the punishment of Fire. (Quran 3:190-191)

Today you have learnt some of the most amazing miracles that science has discovered which we did not know until recently but the Quran mentioned these miracles to us 1400 years ago. This shows that the author of the Quran is none other than Allah Himself.

Workshop

The quiz questions and the exercises are provided to further your understanding. Don't worry if you can't answer all of the questions in the quiz. Try your best to answer as many as you can. You should go back through the chapter to check your answers to these questions.

Quiz 6

1. List some important points we mentioned about scientific miracles in the Quran.
2. What do you understand by 'Heavens with pillars' that Allah mentions in the Quran?
3. What does the Quran say about the Big Bang theory?
4. How will the universe end according to the Quran and Science?

Scientific Miracles in the Universe and on the Earth Mentioned in the Quran

DAY 7

The Light of the Sun and the Moon

In todays lesson you will study the Scientific Miracles in the Universe and on the Earth mentioned in the Quran. In the Quran Allah talks about the Sun and the Moon in several places. Allah describes the light of the Sun and the Moon in the following verses:

وَجَعَلَ ٱلْقَمَرَ فِيهِنَّ نُورًا وَجَعَلَ ٱلشَّمْسَ سِرَاجًا

And [He] has made the Moon a light therein, and made the Sun a lamp (Quran 71:16)

تَبَارَكَ ٱلَّذِى جَعَلَ فِى ٱلسَّمَآءِ بُرُوجًا وَجَعَلَ فِيهَا سِرَأجًا وَقَمَرًا مُّنِيرًا

Blessed is He Who made constellations in the skies, and placed therein a Lamp and a Moon giving light; (Quran 25:61)

هُوَ ٱلَّذِى جَعَلَ ٱلشَّمْسَ ضِيَآءً وَٱلْقَمَرَ نُورًا

He is the One who has made the Sun a glow, and the Moon a light (Quran 10:5)

وَجَعَلْنَا ٱلَّيْلَ وَٱلنَّهَارَ ءَايَتَيْنِ فَمَحَوْنَآ ءَايَةَ ٱلَّيْلِ وَجَعَلْنَآ ءَايَةَ ٱلنَّهَارِ مُبْصِرَةً لِّتَبْتَغُواْ فَضْلاً مِّن

رَّبِّكُمْ وَلِتَعْلَمُواْ عَدَدَ ٱلسِّنِينَ وَٱلْحِسَابَ وَكُلَّ شَيْءٍ فَصَّلْنَٰهُ تَفْصِيلاً

We have made the night and the day two signs, then We made the sign of night marked by darkness and the sign of day bright, so that you may seek grace from your Lord, and that you may know how to number the years and how to compute, and We have expounded everything in detail. (Quran 17:12)

Allah tells us in these verses and many others that the light of the Sun is different to the light of the Moon. The light of the Sun is its own light whereas the light of the Moon is reflected (or borrowed) light. Today science tells us that this is true, that the light of the Moon is reflected light, that is why, in the Quran, the Moon is always described as (نُور – light) and the light of the Sun is always described as

(سِرَاج – lamp) or (ضِيَآء – glow).

The Sun has its own light, and the rays of the Sun burn from the Sun itself. The temperature on the surface of the Sun reaches 6,000°C. The temperature at the centre of the Sun (core temperature) reaches 20,000,000°C (20 million), and solar flares (the giant flames emitted periodically by the Sun) reach up to half a million kilometres out into space. The heat that reaches the Earth from the Sun is less than one ten millionth of one percent of its output. Glory be to Allah Who created the Sun as a great lamp.

The Sun and the Moon have Fixed Courses

Allah says in the Quran:

ٱلشَّمْسُ وَٱلْقَمَرُ بِحُسْبَانٍ

The Sun and the Moon are (bound) by a (fixed) calculation. (Quran 55:5)

Allah tells us that the Sun and the Moon keep to their orbits.

Both the Sun and the Moon have temperatures, sizes, and distances that are accurately established with respect to the Earth.

The Sun is the key to life on Earth, and yet it is incredibly far away. The Sun is 149,600,000 kilometres, (92,955,807 miles) away from us, and this distance from us is so precise that a very small increase or decrease in this distance will affect all life on Earth. Specifically, if the Sun were to come a bit closer than it is now, or get a little larger in its size, we would be set afire, and if it were to shrink or move slightly away from us, then we would freeze.

It is the same with the Moon, the distance between the Moon and the Earth is so accurate that a slight increase or decrease in its distance would drastically affect our lives. If the Moon were to expand a little more or come closer to us, we would be drowned due to flooding by the oceans, and if it were to shrink or move further away, the oceans would disappear from us. Is this not a miracle of precision?

Comets Appearing and Disappearing

Let us look at the topic of Comets in the Quran. Allah says:

$$\text{فَلَآ أُقْسِمُ بِٱلْخُنَّسِ (١٥) ٱلْجَوَارِ ٱلْكُنَّسِ}$$

So, I swear by those (planets) that recede, (and by) the planets that move swiftly, (and) hide themselves. (Quran 81:15-16)

There are many commentaries on this verse, but the most beautiful is one that talks about Comets. Comets are icy objects that release gas and dust as they orbit the Sun. They are made out of dust and ice, and that is why they are also called 'Dirty Snowballs'. They orbit the Sun quite differently to the planets in our solar system. Comets travel swiftly, and their orbits are much longer than those of the planets. As it travels, because it takes a very long time to orbit, it disappears and then, after many years, it returns and we can see it once again. This pattern is the same for every Comet, only the length of time between sightings changes. So, Comets travel very fast and as it orbits it disappears and then comes back again. One particular Comet, the well known Halley's Comet, takes 76 years to complete its orbit around the Sun, and we can only see it for short periods of time.

Who could have told Muhammad ﷺ about these Comets that Allah talks about in the Quran? Every sign and miracle we find tells us that this book is from none other than Allah.

Lord of the <u>two</u> Easts and the <u>two</u> Wests

Allah says in the Quran:

$$رَبُّ ٱلۡمَشۡرِقَيۡنِ وَرَبُّ ٱلۡمَغۡرِبَيۡنِ$$

[He is] Lord of the two Easts and Lord of the two Wests: (Quran 55:17)

Generally we hear of one east and one west, but the Quran talks about two easts and two wests. Where are the two easts and the two wests? Then we find the plural reference to east and west in another place in the Quran. Allah says:

$$فَلَآ أُقۡسِمُ بِرَبِّ ٱلۡمَشَٰرِقِ وَٱلۡمَغَٰرِبِ$$

So I swear by the Lord of easts and wests (Quran 70:40)

So where are these easts and wests, and in the previous verse, two easts and two wests?

The early scholars said that the meaning of the two easts and the two wests means the east in summer and the other east in winter. However, I want you to imagine a scene with me in space. There is a star that has been recently discovered which revolves about two Suns (Alpha Centauri A and Alpha Centauri B). Every day it has two Sunrises and two Sunsets.

There are some stars that revolve about three Suns. Some stars that revolve about four Suns and even five Suns. The maximum number they have discovered so far is a star that revolves about six Suns. These are the easts and wests that Allah mentions in the Quran.

What the earlier scholars said is also correct, but I want you to consider this verse of the Quran from a different angle.

The Size of an Atom

Allah says in the Quran:

وَمَا يَعْزُبُ عَن رَّبِّكَ مِن مِّثْقَالِ ذَرَّةٍ فِي ٱلْأَرْضِ وَلَا فِي ٱلسَّمَآءِ وَلَآ أَصْغَرَ مِن ذَٰلِكَ وَلَآ أَكْبَرَ إِلَّا فِى كِتَٰبٍ مُّبِينٍ

Nor is hidden from thy Lord (so much as) the weight of an atom on the Earth or in Heaven. And not the least and not the greatest of these things but are recorded in a clear Record. (Quran 10:61)

The Arabs used the word (ذَرَّة – atom) to mean 'the smallest thing', and for many years mankind did not know of anything smaller than an atom. It was not until 1939 when this topic was discussed in the University of Berlin that scientists discovered that there is indeed something smaller than an atom. Look! The Quran tells us 1400 years ago that there is something smaller than an atom.

The weight of an atom is 2 over one million million millionth of a gram. Can one even begin to imagine the minute size of something so light in weight? An atom is formed of electrons, protons and neutrons. In the nucleus of an atom there are neutrons and protons. The nucleus is the centre of an atom and electrons orbit the nucleus.

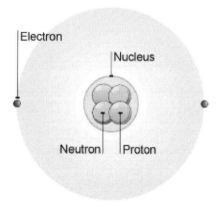

Diagram of a Helium Atom

This diagram shows a Helium atom. The size of the electron when compared to the atom is incredibly small. To understand the size, imagine that you are sitting in a room, the room is the size of an atom and the electrons are like the particles of dust in this room. As the dust is to the room, so is the electron to an atom.

The Quark

There is something even smaller than an electron, which is called a Quark. And one of the amazing things about the creation of Allah is that everything in this universe: animals, trees, plants, humans, planets, stars, the moon … Everything in this universe is created from the Quark. The whole universe is One and One God created this universe. Amazing, wonderful, miraculous beauty, there is one particle, the Quark, and everything is composed of the Quark.

We have said that a Quark is smaller than an electron, but how small is it in comparison to an electron? In order to understand the sizes of these two miniscule particles, imagine that you are on the top of a twenty storey building, and on the ground below you see an orange. This is the size of a Quark compared to the size of an electron. Like an orange as you see it from the top of a twenty storey building.

Day and Night

Allah says in the Quran:

هُوَ ٱلَّذِى جَعَلَ لَكُمُ ٱلَّيْلَ لِتَسْكُنُوا۟ فِيهِ وَٱلنَّهَارَ مُبْصِرًا

He is the One Who made for you the night, so that you may have rest in it, and (made) the day to see. (Quran 10:67)

يُغْشِى ٱلَّيْلَ ٱلنَّهَارَ يَطْلُبُهُ حَثِيثًا

He covers the day with the night that pursues it swiftly. (Quran 7:54)

وَهُوَ ٱلَّذِى جَعَلَ لَكُمُ ٱلَّيْلَ لِبَاسًا

And He it is Who makes the night as a covering for you (Quran 25:47)

These are some of the verses in which Allah talks about night and day; there are many more, but I have selected these few. Some of these verses we read many times over but we forget to reflect. When we understand a bit more of the amazing universe then we will better understand these verses.

Allah says, (يُغْشِى ٱلَّيْلَ ٱلنَّهَارَ) which means He covers the day with the night. i.e. the night covers the day. Let us look at the day and how the night has covered it. During the day, when we see daylight, what do we see when we look at the sky? We see day. But above daylight there is darkness. The Sun is there, we can see the Sun, we can see daylight, but above daylight there is darkness. This is not a theory, this is an established scientific fact. People have seen this with their own eyes, that on the surface of the earth there is day and on top of this day there is night. The day is, in fact, surrounded by night. Allah says: (يُغْشِى ٱلَّيْلَ ٱلنَّهَارَ) the night covers the day. And Allah says: (جَعَلَ لَكُمُ ٱلَّيْلَ لِبَاسًا) He has made for you the night as a covering, as in the night covers the day.

In another place Allah talks about the day and He says:

وَٱلنَّهَارَ مُبْصِرًا

And (Allah has made) the day to see. (Quran 10:67)

'Daylight' is an earthly thing. It does not exist anywhere in the universe other than here on Earth. What about the other planets; Mercury, Venus, Mars, and so forth? They do not have daylight. There is only darkness and therefore night on them. What about the Sun? Does it not give the other planets daylight? The Sun exists, and is visible on the planets, but they see the Sun the same way we on Earth see the Stars at night. The Planets see the Sun, but they do not have any daylight. So suppose you were on Mars, you would see the luminous Sun in the sky as a big bright Star, but surrounded by night. There is no 'daytime' except for us here on this Earth.

The Quran gives an amazing description when challenging the disbelievers and the people about ascending through the atmosphere.

وَلَوْ فَتَحْنَا عَلَيْهِم بَابًا مِّنَ ٱلسَّمَآءِ فَظَلُّواْ فِيهِ يَعْرُجُونَ (١٤) لَقَالُوٓاْ إِنَّمَا سُكِّرَتْ أَبْصَٰرُنَا بَلْ

نَحْنُ قَوْمٌ مَّسْحُورُونَ

Even if We opened out to them a gate from Heaven, and they were to continue (all day) ascending therein, They would only say: "Our eyes have been intoxicated: nay, we have been bewitched by sorcery." (Quran 15:14-15)

Before we discuss this verse, let us first, look at some of the words it contains: (ظَلُّواْ) is a word that is used for something that occurs during the day. If the thing occurs during night then you will use the word (بَاتُوا).

(يَعْرُجُ) means to ascend with inclination or in curve. That's why one who walks stooped or bent over is called (أَعْرَجَ) in Arabic. So the word (يَعْرُجُونَ) has two meanings. It has the meaning of ascending and it also has the meaning of inclination.

I want you to do an exercise with me. Close your eyes for a few seconds. What do you see when you close your eyes? You see darkness. Isn't this always true? When you close your eyes, all you see is darkness?

Allah asks, if they start to ascend through this gate in the skies, what will happen? Allah uses the word (ظَلُّواْ), which means that this ascension is not during the night, it is during the day. If Allah was talking about nighttime, Allah would have said (فَبَاتُواْ فِيهِ يَعْرُجُونَ) but He is talking about ascending during the day. Once they ascend to the skies and they pass the atmosphere, what will they see? They will see darkness, night. What will they say? They will say سُكِّرَتْ أَبْصَارُنَا" - Our eyes have been intoxicated). From where did this night come? From where did this darkness come? We came from daylight." They would say, "This is magic, darkness and night during the day?" This would be the scene in the upper atmosphere upon seeing complete darkness. This verse is describing a daytime event. Daytime, daylight, exists only here on Earth, not in the upper atmosphere or beyond it.

Next time you read these verses ponder over this comprehensive description that Muhammad ﷺ could only have received from Allah through revelation, because

120

these things were not known to mankind until they started sending rockets into space.

The Gate in the Sky

There is another miracle that I find amazing in this verse. Allah says: (بَابًا مِّنَ ٱلسَّمَآءِ) 'a gate from the Heaven'. Today science tells us that spacecraft and space shuttles when they want to ascend they cannot reach up into the upper atmosphere from just anywhere. They must enter from one of a few specific places. These serve as passageways for the space shuttles. The upper atmosphere has gates, which are the only access to the stratosphere. If you enter the stratosphere from any other place than these specific ones, you will die. That's why Allah said: (بَابًا مِّنَ ٱلسَّمَآءِ) a gate from the Heaven.

You Can Only Enter the Stratosphere with Inclination

Further Allah mentions that the ascending path into the stratosphere must be curved. You cannot enter the stratosphere in a straight trajectory. It is important for the space shuttles to climb through the atmosphere following a curved trajectory.

That is why Allah did not use the word (يَصْعُدُوْن) which means ascending, He used the word (يَعْرُجُونَ) which is ascending with inclination. Glory be to Allah Who selected each and every word with truth in the Quran.

Signs on the Earth

Let us now discuss some of the Miracles on the Earth mentioned in the Quran. Allah says:

$$وَفِى ٱلْأَرْضِ ءَايَـٰتٌ لِّلْمُوقِنِينَ$$

In the Earth, there are signs for those who (seek truth to) believe (Quran 51:20)

In the same way that there are miracles and signs of Allah in the universe, there are signs and miracles of Allah on the Earth. In this part of the section we are going to study some of the miracles related to the Earth.

The Barrier between two Bodies of Flowing Water

Allah mentions amongst His signs on the Earth:

$$أَمَّن جَعَلَ ٱلْأَرْضَ قَرَارًا وَجَعَلَ خِلَٰلَهَآ أَنْهَٰرًا وَجَعَلَ لَهَا رَوَٰسِىَ وَجَعَلَ بَيْنَ ٱلْبَحْرَيْنِ حَاجِزًا$$

$$أَءِلَٰهٌ مَّعَ ٱللَّهِ بَلْ أَكْثَرُهُمْ لَا يَعْلَمُونَ$$

Or, who has made the Earth firm to live in; made rivers in its midst; set thereon mountains immovable; and made a separating bar between the two bodies of flowing water? (Can there be another) god besides Allah? Nay most of them know not. (Quran 27:61)

In this verse Allah talks about many of His signs on the Earth. We will discuss one of them in particular. Allah says that He 'has put a barrier between the two bodies of flowing water'.

Firstly, let us define what a barrier is. A barrier is prevention between two things with a barrier between the two. So Allah is saying that there is a barrier between the two seas. Allah repeats this same message in another verse:

$$مَرَجَ ٱلْبَحْرَيْنِ يَلْتَقِيَانِ (١٩) بَيْنَهُمَا بَرْزَخٌ لَّا يَبْغِيَانِ$$

He has let free the two bodies of flowing water, meeting together: Between them is a Barrier which they do not transgress: (Quran 55:19-20)

In yet another verse Allah says:

$$وَهُوَ ٱلَّذِى مَرَجَ ٱلْبَحْرَيْنِ هَٰذَا عَذْبٌ فُرَاتٌ وَهَٰذَا مِلْحٌ أُجَاجٌ وَجَعَلَ بَيْنَهُمَا بَرْزَخًا وَحِجْرًا$$

$$مَّحْجُورًا$$

It is He Who has let free the two bodies of flowing water: one palatable and sweet and the other salt and bitter; yet has He made a barrier between them, a partition that is forbidden to be passed. (Quran 25:53)

The Quran refers to barriers in the seas. When we go to the sea, do we find barriers? It was not until 1873 when the historic HMS Challenger Expedition set out to discover what lay beneath the surface of the world's oceans that they found

something amazing. They discovered that there are lines that separate the two seas. A person looking at the sea's surface will not be able to see these lines. But during their exploration, they discovered that there are separate colours; that the two bodies of water have different densities, and even the temperatures of the two 'waters' differ. This barrier starts from the top of the sea and continues all the way down to the bottom of the sea. In some seas the barrier is there for about one kilometre in the water, and as the water moves this barrier moves but the two waters do not mix. This phenomenon is also present in the Arabian Gulf and the Gulf of Oman.

Who taught this to Muhammad ﷺ when he had never been to sea or travelled on a ship? Who described this in the Quran, when this phenomenon cannot be seen without the use of modern technology? Today this is a scientific fact that there are barriers between two bodies of flowing water.

The Zone of Debouchment

In Surah Furqan Allah – besides talking about the barrier – Allah further says:

$$\text{وَجَعَلَ بَيْنَهُمَا بَرْزَخًا وَحِجْرًا مَّحْجُورًا}$$

He made a barrier between them, a partition that is forbidden to be passed. (Quran 25:53)

What is this partition that is forbidden to be passed? The word (حِجْرًا) means 'a partition'.

(حِجْرًا مَّحْجُورًا) means 'a place where it is forbidden to enter or exit'. What is this verse referring to? Scientists have found that when the water of the sea mixes with the water of the river then this creates a third distinct environment. This third zone is neither a part of the sea nor a part of the river. It even has its own designation, it is called a 'debouchment'. It is a distinct environment from both the river and the sea in terms of its saltiness and the nature of its inhabitants, which are completely different.

Scientists then realised another amazing thing, they discovered that the creatures that lived in the river died if they entered this zone. Similarly, the creatures living in the sea also died if they entered this zone. The same holds true for the creatures living in the debouchment, they cannot live in either the sea or the river environment. Is this not what Allah describes in this verse, a partition that it is forbidden to pass? Paraphrasing the verse: It is prohibited for any living creatures to enter or exit this zone for they will die.

Summary

Today, you have learnt about some of the amazing scientific miracles in the Universe and on the Earth that are mentioned in the Quran. You have learnt about the night and the day, which exists only here on the Earth. You have learnt about the Sun and the Moon running on their fixed courses. You have learnt about the Stars that have two Sunsets and two Sunrises, and that the Quran mentions this phenomenon 1400 years ago. When did Muhammad ﷺ voyage the universe to discover these phenomena? There were no microscopes or telescopes in his time. Every single miracle proves to us that the author of this book is none other than our Creator, Allah.

You also learnt about the Zone of Debouchment that the Quran talks about, as well as the barrier between two bodies of flowing water.

Allah gave previous Prophets Miracles, but those miracles were intended for the immediate benefit of those people present to witness them at the time. Allah wanted to give us signs and miracles 'for all time'.

وَكَأَيِّن مِّنْ ءَايَةٍ فِى ٱلسَّمَٰوَٰتِ وَٱلْأَرْضِ يَمُرُّونَ عَلَيْهَا وَهُمْ عَنْهَا مُعْرِضُونَ

How many a sign there is in the Heavens and the Earth, which they pass by and they are heedless to them. (Quran 12:105)

There are many signs, but we pass by them, and we ignore them. Do not remain amongst the ignorant after seeing these signs.

إِنَّمَا يَسْتَجِيبُ ٱلَّذِينَ يَسْمَعُونَ وَٱلْمَوْتَىٰ يَبْعَثُهُمُ ٱللَّهُ ثُمَّ إِلَيْهِ يُرْجَعُونَ

Only those respond who listen (to seek the truth). As for the dead, Allah shall raise them, after which they shall be returned to Him. (Quran 6:36)

Workshop

The quiz questions and the exercises are provided to further your understanding. Don't worry if you can't answer all of the questions in the quiz. Try your best to answer as many as you can. You should go back through the chapter to check your answers to these questions.

Quiz 7

1. What does the Quran say about the light of the Sun and the light of the Moon?
2. What does 'the Sun and the Moon run on their fixed courses' mean?
3. What is the meaning of 'two easts and two wests'?
4. What is the Zone of Debouchment that both the Quran and science indicate?

7

Scientific Miracles on the Earth mentioned in the Quran

DAY 8

The Deeds of the Non-Believers

In today's lesson, you will study some more of the scientific miracles on the Earth that are mentioned in the Quran. You will learn some of the miracles related to the seas and oceans. Allah says:

وَٱلَّذِينَ كَفَرُوٓاْ أَعْمَٰلُهُمْ كَسَرَابٍۭ بِقِيعَةٍ يَحْسَبُهُ ٱلظَّمْـَٔانُ مَآءً حَتَّىٰٓ إِذَا جَآءَهُۥ لَمْ يَجِدْهُ شَيْـًٔا وَوَجَدَ ٱللَّهَ عِندَهُۥ فَوَفَّىٰهُ حِسَابَهُۥ وَٱللَّهُ سَرِيعُ ٱلْحِسَابِ

> As for those who disbelieve, their deeds are like a mirage in a desert plain, which a thirsty person deems to be water, until when he comes to it, he finds it nothing, and finds (the decree of) Allah with him, so He pays him his account in full. Allah is swift at reckoning. (Quran 24:39)

(سَرَاب) is mirage, it is an optical illusion promising water ahead when the weather is hot, but when you get there you realize that there was no water. When you get there you find it was only an illusion without any reality.

This verse is a description of the deeds of the non-believers. Their deeds are like a mirage. A non-believer may do good deeds, he gets tired, does more good deeds, and gets more tired; and he thinks that he will get his reward. On the Day of Judgement he does not get any reward because he had no Iman (faith). All of this hard work that he did was just an illusion. What will he find instead? He will find Allah.

Allah continues and gives another example of the deeds of the non-believers. Allah says:

أَوْ كَظُلُمَٰتٍ فِى بَحْرٍ لُّجِّىٍّ يَغْشَىٰهُ مَوْجٌ مِّن فَوْقِهِۦ مَوْجٌ مِّن فَوْقِهِۦ سَحَابٌ ظُلُمَٰتٌۢ بَعْضُهَا فَوْقَ بَعْضٍ إِذَآ أَخْرَجَ يَدَهُۥ لَمْ يَكَدْ يَرَىٰهَا

> Or (their deeds) are like layers of darkness in a vast deep sea overwhelmed by a wave, above which there is another wave, above which there are clouds – layers of darkness, one above the other. When one puts forth his hand, he can hardly see it. (Quran 24:40)

Allah compares the deeds of the non-believers with intense darkness. There is no light in their deeds, the deeds of the non-believers are like the darkness in a deep

8

127

ocean. Firstly, how did Muhammad ﷺ know that inside the ocean is darkness? We know from his biography that he never travelled across the sea. And those who did travel by sea, or work as fishermen or divers in his time, they were not able to go deeper than 20-30 meters, and at a depth of 30 meters there is still light, and not complete darkness. Complete darkness in the Ocean only exists when you reach 1000 meters or 1 kilometre in depth. Going this deep was not possible for human beings until the invention of submarines. If a person tried to swim so deep in the ocean without a diving suit, or outside of a submarine, he would drown.

And the verse talks about more than this darkness. The verse says (ظُلُمَٰتٌ), meaning darknesses. Let me ask you a question, suppose you switch your lights off in your bedroom and close the doors, how many 'darknesses' do you see? You see one darkness. Allah used the plural of darkness, as in more than one darkness. Some scholars suggested that Allah used the plural of darkness to show the intensity of the darkness. But this is not true. Allah used the plural form of darkness because He meant more than one darkness. If we were to agree for the sake of argument that Allah used the plural form of darkness to show the intensity of darkness, then when Allah says 'layers of darkness, one above the other', how do you understand this? Intense darkness upon intense darkness? It is meaningless.

Mankind did not know the meaning of this 'more than one darkness', until science discovered something amazing which occurs only in the deep ocean. It only occurs in the depths of the ocean, below a vast amount of water.

If you look at a light, what colour is it? It is white. If you put white light through a prism then light 'breaks down' into seven colours:

The seven colours are: red, orange, yellow, green, blue, indigo, violet. The scientists discovered that at a depth of 10 meters, the red light disappears. Therefore if a diver is 25 metres down in a deep ocean and gets wounded, he is not able to see the redness of his blood, because red cannot be seen at this depth. Similarly orange rays are absorbed at 30 to 50 metres, yellow at 50 to 100 metres, green at 100 to 200

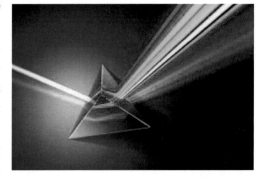

metres, and blue beyond 200 metres. (Oceans, Elder and Pernetta, p. 27. 1 2)

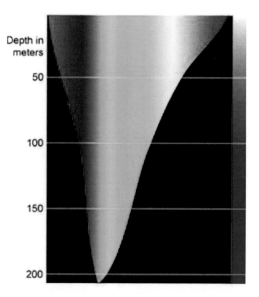

Due to the successive disappearance of each colour, one layer after another, the ocean progressively becomes darker, i.e. darkness gets deeper as layers of light are removed. Below 1000 meters deep there is complete darkness. This is what the Quran says: (ظُلُمَـٰتٌ بَعْضُهَا فَوْقَ بَعْضٍ) layers of darkness, one above the other. Furthermore, Allah said this only happens in the deep ocean, because this phenomenon occurs nowhere else except in the deep ocean.

Internal Waves

This verse in addition to the layers of darkness in the deep ocean, it also talks about the 'Internal Waves'.

يَغْشَـٰهُ مَوْجٌ مِّن فَوْقِهِۦ مَوْجٌ مِّن فَوْقِهِۦ سَحَابٌ

> Overwhelmed by a wave, above which there is another wave, above which there are clouds. (Quran 24:40)

What covers the ocean? It is a wave, above which there is another wave, above which there are clouds. So where is the cloud? It is in the atmosphere. The verse says that under this cloud there is a wave, and under this wave there is another wave, and under this wave is the deep ocean.

It was not until 1900 that scientists discovered internal waves. When you see waves on the surface of the sea, there is internal movement within these waves. So the movement of surface waves are driven by internal forces. They discovered that other internal waves are travelling exactly opposite to the surface waves. So if the surface waves are moving towards the right then these other internal waves are moving towards the left. There are waves on the surface and at depth too. These internal waves extend up to hundreds of meters, as do the waves on the surface.

8

This phenomenon is comprised within the meaning of (يَغْشَىٰهُ مَوْجٌ مِّن فَوْقِهِۦ مَوْجٌ) 'overwhelmed by a wave, above which there is another wave'.

وَٱلَّذِينَ كَفَرُوا۟ بِـَٔايَٰتِ ٱللَّهِ أُو۟لَٰٓئِكَ هُمُ ٱلْخَٰسِرُونَ

As for those who have rejected the verses of Allah, it is they who are the losers. (Quran 39:63)

The people who continue in disbelief of Allah after these signs, then they are the losers, because this is not the work of a human being. It is impossible that a human being could have referred to these matters 1400 years ago.

Clouds - Types of Clouds Mentioned in the Quran

Allah talks about clouds and their types in the Quran. We will look at three different verses that talk about clouds then we will discuss each type in details. Allah says:

أَلَمْ تَرَ أَنَّ ٱللَّهَ يُزْجِى سَحَابًا ثُمَّ يُؤَلِّفُ بَيْنَهُ ثُمَّ يَجْعَلُهُ رُكَامًا فَتَرَى ٱلْوَدْقَ يَخْرُجُ مِنْ خِلَلِهِ

وَيُنَزِّلُ مِنَ ٱلسَّمَآءِ مِن جِبَالٍ فِيهَا مِنْ بَرَدٍ فَيُصِيبُ بِهِ مَن يَشَآءُ وَيَصْرِفُهُ عَن مَّن يَشَآءُ

يَكَادُ سَنَا بَرْقِهِ يَذْهَبُ بِٱلْأَبْصَٰرِ

Do you not realize that Allah drives the clouds, then joins them together, then turns them into a heap? Then you see the rain coming out from their midst. He sends down from the sky mountains (of clouds) having hail in them, then He afflicts with it whomsoever He wills and turns it away from whomsoever He wills. The flash of its lightning seems to snatch away the eyes. (Quran 24:43)

ٱللَّهُ ٱلَّذِى يُرْسِلُ ٱلرِّيَٰحَ فَتُثِيرُ سَحَابًا فَيَبْسُطُهُ فِى ٱلسَّمَآءِ كَيْفَ يَشَآءُ وَيَجْعَلُهُ كِسَفًا فَتَرَى

ٱلْوَدْقَ يَخْرُجُ مِنْ خِلَلِهِ فَإِذَآ أَصَابَ بِهِ مَن يَشَآءُ مِنْ عِبَادِهِ إِذَا هُمْ يَسْتَبْشِرُونَ

Allah is the One Who sends the winds, so they stir up a cloud, then He spreads it in the sky however He wills, and makes it (split) into pieces. Then you see the rain coming out from its midst. So, once He makes it reach those whom He wills from His slaves, they start rejoicing. (Quran 30:48)

وَأَنزَلْنَا مِنَ ٱلْمُعْصِرَاتِ مَآءً ثَجَّاجًا ﴿١٤﴾ لِّنُخْرِجَ بِهِ حَبًّا وَنَبَاتًا ﴿١٥﴾ وَجَنَّاتٍ أَلْفَافًا

And We have sent down abundant water from the rain-laden clouds, So that We bring out therewith grain and vegetation, And thick gardens. (Quran 78:14-16)

All these verses talk about rain and the growing of plants, and the goodness rain brings. This is what the early commentators of the Quran noted. However, with recent discoveries we find something much more amazing than this in these verses.

There are twelve different types of cloud. In fact clouds have been categorised into eighty different types! But generally clouds are divided into three main categories.

1. Cumulus, also known as Cumuliform Clouds

2. Cirrus, also known as Stratiform Clouds

3. Tornadoes, also known as Hurricanes

These three verses refer to these three main types of cloud. Mankind divided clouds into these categories in the 20th century. Yet Allah told us about these categories 1400 years ago through Muhammad ﷺ. Not only did He tell us about these categories, He also gave us descriptions of these three types of cloud.

Cumulus – Cumuliform Clouds

These clouds are most impressive in height but rather less so in breadth; the horizontal expanse of this type of cloud being relatively small by comparison. They only extend to between 8 and 10 kilometres. Vertically, however, they go upwards in layers, sometimes reaching 20 kilometres in height. They are similar to mountains in the way they rise from their bases to immense heights. So a cumuliform cloud goes upwards in layers, 'then [He] turns them into a heap' until it looks like a mountain.'

Another point that the Quran mentions is that this type of cloud produces thunder and lightning. This phenomenon is specific to cumuliform clouds. That is why in the verse (Quran 24:43) quoted, Allah mentions lightning. Therefore if you ever see lightning then you are looking at a cumuliform cloud. That is why Allah say:

يَكَادُ سَنَا بَرْقِهِ يَذْهَبُ بِٱلْأَبْصَرِ

The flash of its lightning seems to snatch away the eyes. (Quran 24:43)

This is a precise description of the first type of cloud 'Cumulus – Cumuliform Clouds'.

Cirrus – Stratiform Clouds

In contrast to the first verse, in the second verse Allah says:

ٱللَّهُ ٱلَّذِى يُرْسِلُ ٱلرِّيَٰحَ فَتُثِيرُ سَحَابًا فَيَبْسُطُهُ فِى ٱلسَّمَآءِ كَيْفَ يَشَآءُ وَيَجْعَلُهُ كِسَفًا فَتَرَى ٱلْوَدْقَ يَخْرُجُ مِنْ خِلَٰلِهِ فَإِذَآ أَصَابَ بِهِ مَن يَشَآءُ مِنْ عِبَادِهِ إِذَا هُمْ يَسْتَبْشِرُونَ

Allah is the One Who sends the winds, so they stir up a cloud, then He spreads it in the sky however he wills, and makes it (split) into pieces. Then you see the rain coming out from its midst. So, once He makes it reach those whom He wills of His slaves, they start rejoicing. (Quran 30:48)

In the first verse, Allah said that He makes clouds in layers, in the second verse Allah says that He spreads the clouds in the sky. Stratiform cloud can spread up to 200 kilometres. Just one cloud can reach up to 200 kilometres across! So this is the first difference between cumuliform and stratiform clouds. Cumuliform cloud go upwards in layers, stratiform cloud spreads horizontally.

Another difference is that stratiform cloud does not produce thunder and lightning, whereas cumuliform cloud does. Now if you look at the verse (Quran 30:48) I am asking you, did Allah mention lightning in this verse? Did Allah mention thunder? No, why? Because this is exactly the definition of stratiform clouds, that there is no cold in them and neither is there thunder and lightning. Glory to Allah!

The Quran makes another important point in the above two verses. Stratiform clouds bring light rain, whereas cumuliform clouds bring heavy rain, which may be harmful and can cause floods and so forth. This is why when Allah talks about the cumuliform clouds He says:

$$فَيُصِيبُ بِهِۦ مَن يَشَآءُ وَيَصۡرِفُهُۥ عَن مَّن يَشَآءُ$$

Then He afflicts with it whomsoever He wills and turns it away from whomsoever He wills. (Quran 24:43)

In contrast to this, when Allah talks about stratiform clouds, He says:

$$فَإِذَآ أَصَابَ بِهِۦ مَن يَشَآءُ مِنۡ عِبَادِهِۦٓ إِذَا هُمۡ يَسۡتَبۡشِرُونَ$$

So, once He makes it reach those whom He wills of His slaves, they start rejoicing. (Quran 30:48)

Because the kind of rain that stratiform clouds produce is light, it is not harmful. The rain that is harmful and can cause damage is the type of rain that is produced by cumuliform clouds.

Tornadoes – Hurricanes

The third verse that we mentioned, tells us about the third type of cloud, Tornadoes. The cities that have been hit most frequently by Tornadoes, are Texas and Oklahoma City. Tornadoes are exactly as the Quran describes them, (مَآءً ثَجَّاجًا

– abundant water), the rain pours down like a waterfall. If you are travelling in a car during a tornado, you cannot see the car in front of you because of the water pouring down on your car windscreen. Tornadoes normally occur in tropical latitudes and as a result, plants and trees grow prolifically. You will see many lakes, which are surrounded by trees in these tropical places. This is exactly how the verse describes tornadoes and says:

$$\text{لِنُخْرِجَ بِهِ حَبًّا وَنَبَاتًا (١٥) وَجَنَّتٍ أَلْفَافًا}$$

So that We bring out therewith grain and vegetation, And thick gardens. (Quran 78:15-16)

Allah does not mention the growth of trees and plants when He speaks about cumuliform clouds or stratiform clouds. Who sent Muhammad ﷺ to tropical places or Oklahoma City? It is Allah Who sends the winds, it is He Who sends rain with goodness. Glory to Allah, is there any God besides Allah?

وَمَن يُرْسِلُ ٱلرِّيَاحَ بُشْرًا بَيْنَ يَدَىْ رَحْمَتِهِۦ أَءِلَٰهٌ مَّعَ ٱللَّهِ تَعَٰلَى ٱللَّهُ عَمَّا يُشْرِكُونَ

And who sends the winds bearing good news before His mercy? Is there any god along with Allah? Allah is far higher than the partners they ascribe to Him. (Quran 27:63)

The Miracle of the Mountain in the Quran

Amongst the miracles that Allah mentions in the Quran is the miracle of the mountain. Allah describes mountains in the following verses:

وَٱلْجِبَالَ أَوْتَادًا

And the mountains as pegs? (Quran 78:7)

وَجَعَلْنَا فِيهَا رَوَاسِىَ شَٰمِخَٰتٍ

And made therein mountains standing firm, lofty (in stature) (Quran 77:27)

أَمَّن جَعَلَ ٱلْأَرْضَ قَرَارًا وَجَعَلَ خِلَٰلَهَآ أَنْهَٰرًا وَجَعَلَ لَهَا رَوَاسِىَ وَجَعَلَ بَيْنَ ٱلْبَحْرَيْنِ حَاجِزًا أَءِلَٰهٌ مَّعَ ٱللَّهِ بَلْ أَكْثَرُهُمْ لَا يَعْلَمُونَ

Or, who has made the Earth firm to live in; made rivers in its midst; set thereon mountains immovable; and made a separating bar between the two bodies of flowing water? (Can there be another) god besides Allah? Nay most of them know not. (Quran 27:61)

وَأَلْقَىٰ فِى ٱلْأَرْضِ رَوَاسِىَ أَن تَمِيدَ بِكُمْ

He set on the Earth, Mountains standing firm lest it should shake with you; (Quran 31:10)

In these verses, Allah uses the following words when describing the mountains:

(رَوَاسِىَ) which means to become firm.

(أَوْتَادًا) means pegs. Tent pegs hold the tent firm in its place, and only a small part of the peg shows, the majority of it is in the ground. Similarly, mountains are like tent pegs, you see only a small part of it, the majority of it is underground.

Then Allah says (أَن تَمِيدَ بِكُمْ) 'lest it should shake with you'.

Mankind did not understand the meaning of mountains becoming firm and mountains as tent pegs until 1956, when science discovered that the mountains that we see have deep roots which extend a long way below the base of the mountain. This is similar to an iceberg, how we see only a small portion at the top, while most of it remains hidden underwater. So, for every mountain we see only a small part of it is above ground, and it's roots beneath the ground can be up to 4 ½ times bigger than what you see above the surface.

Mountains give stability to the Earth so that it does not shake, and this has been confirmed as an established fact, it is not a theory, it is a fact that mountains protect the Earth from getting too close to the Sun. If this precise and accurate stabilising effect of the mountains were not there, the Earth would be gradually pulled into the Sun.

Then scholars reflected over these verses and found that whenever Allah talks about mountains He then talks about water, rivers and streams. Today after research we have come to know that the sweetest water is that which comes out from the mountains. This is why Allah linked mountains with water, streams and rivers.

The Lowest Point on Earth

الٓمٓ (١) غُلِبَتِ ٱلرُّومُ (٢) فِىٓ أَدۡنَى ٱلۡأَرۡضِ وَهُم مِّنۢ بَعۡدِ غَلَبِهِمۡ سَيَغۡلِبُونَ (٣) فِى بِضۡعِ سِنِينَ

Alif Lam Mim. The Roman Empire has been defeated In a land close by; but they, (even) after (this) defeat of theirs, will soon be victorious Within a few years. (Quran 30:1-4)

When the commentators of the Quran commented on the verse (أَدۡنَى ٱلۡأَرۡضِ – land close by) they said that this place refers to Palestine because (أَدۡنَى – close by) means (أَقۡرَب – nearest). And the nearest place to the Arab land is Palestine. But the word (أَدۡنَى) does not only mean (أَقۡرَب – nearest), it is also the opposite of (أَعۡلَى – highest), so in this context the meaning will be the lowest point. So, when the Quran speaks about (أَدۡنَى ٱلۡأَرۡضِ), besides referring to the closest place, it also refers to 'the lowest point on Earth'. Mankind did not know that the lowest point on Earth is in Palestine, until they accurately measured the altitude of the Dead Sea, and discovered that it is the lowest point on Earth. The lowest point on Earth is 392 metres below sea-level.

Who taught Muhammad ﷺ that the lowest point on Earth is in Palestine? This is nothing but a revelation from Allah.

138

You cannot Escape Allah in the Earth nor in the Heaven

أُوْلَٰٓئِكَ لَمْ يَكُونُوا۟ مُعْجِزِينَ فِى ٱلْأَرْضِ

These could not escape on the Earth (Quran 11:20)

وَمَآ أَنتُم بِمُعْجِزِينَ فِى ٱلْأَرْضِ وَلَا فِى ٱلسَّمَآءِ

And ye cannot escape in the Earth nor in the Heaven (Quran 29:22)

The first verse says that you cannot escape Allah on the Earth; the second verse says that you cannot escape Allah neither on the Earth nor in the Heavens. Why does Allah add 'Heaven' in the second verse?

When Allah talks about the people at the time of Muhammad ﷺ and the people before Muhammad ﷺ, Allah doesn't mention the Heavens because they did not have the technology to reach the skies. In the second verse, because Allah knew that people in the future would be able to travel the skies and voyage in space due to advancements in technology, power generation and sources, rockets and space shuttles, Allah added the word 'Heavens' in the second verse. In addition to this, Allah also began the verse with (أَنتُم) which means 'you people'. Here, Allah is talking to the people of the present day, because today we can go into space. In the previous verse when Allah was talking about the earlier people, mankind was not able to go into space, Allah used the word (أُوْلَٰٓئِكَ) 'these people', because they did not know how to enter space, whereas you, you will have the necessary knowledge to enable space travel. Therefore 'you people' cannot escape Allah neither on the Earth nor in the Heavens.

Summary

Today, You learnt about the layers of darkness that the Quran mentions in the deep ocean. You also learnt about the different types of cloud that science has categorized for us today, but these categories, with their descriptions, were revealed 1400 years ago in the Quran.

8

The Quran tells us of miracles in space, in the universe, and on the Earth to emphasize one thing, and that is that there is One Creator, Allah, and He Alone deserves to be worshipped *and no one else*.

Workshop

The quiz questions and the exercises are provided to further your understanding. Don't worry if you can't answer all of the questions in the quiz. Try your best to answer as many as you can. You should go back through the chapter to check your answers to these questions.

Quiz 8

1. What are the layers of darkness that the Quran describes in the deep ocean?
2. What does the Quran tell us about the different types of clouds?
3. What does the Quran say about the mountains?
4. What does the Quran reveal about the lowest point on Earth?

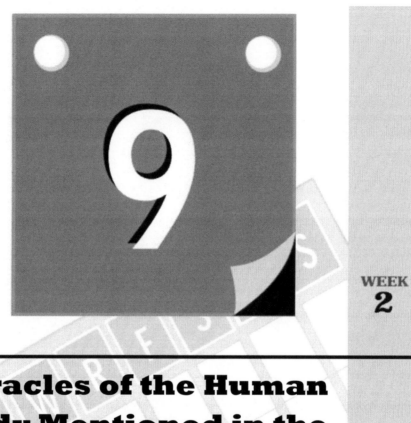

Miracles of the Human Body Mentioned in the Quran

DAY 9

9

Introduction to the Miracles of the Human Body

In the previous chapters we have examined miracles and signs on the Earth and in the Universe. There are a lot more signs and miracles than those we have presented to you. But the purpose of this book is to open the door for you so that you can build upon this foundation that we are providing for you. For this chapter I want to take you to a new world, the world of the human being and the human body. Allah says in the Quran:

وَفِي أَنفُسِكُمْ ۚ أَفَلَا تُبْصِرُونَ

As also in your own selves: will ye not then see? (Quran 51:21)

The design of the human body is an amazing creation by Allah. One of the best documentaries I have watched on this topic is called 'The incredible machine' (1975; dirs Rosten, Irwin; Spiegel, Ed), it is approximately an hour long documentary. Firstly, I will mention a few points from this documentary, then I will take you to the verses from the Quran that address this topic.

The Eyes

We will start by looking at the eyes that Allah has given to us. The miracle of Allah in the eyes is that 90% of the information that a human being gets is through his eyes. Amongst the miracle of the eyes is to blink. A human being blinks his eyes every six seconds, which is approximately ten blinks per minute. When a person reads, the light hits the rods and cones of the retina, which then is converted to an electrical signal. That is then relayed to the brain via the optic nerve. The brain then translates the electrical signals into the images we see.

Retina: This is where more than one hundred and twenty million photoreceptors convert light into electrical impulses before sending them off to the brain for processing.

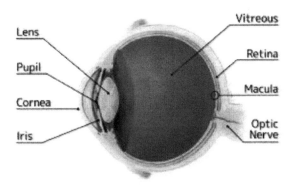

Tears: Allah has created the tears. These tears, besides lubricating and protecting the cornea also clean and wash the eyes.

The Skin

The Skin is an amazing creation of Allah. In one square inch of skin there are 625 sweat glands and 90 oil glands. There are also 19 million cells and 19 feet of blood vessels in every single square inch. This is undoubtedly by the power of Allah.

The Skin is the body's largest organ and a closer look provides a different landscape. Our outer skin is nothing but dead cells with countless bumps and holes and if you look closer you will find hundreds and thousands of bacteria inhabit every square inch of us.

If we were to peel our skin off and lay it flat, the average person's skin would cover some 18 square feet and weigh about 6 pounds.

Around us we see people of different sizes, shapes, colours and textures but on some level we all inhabit the same skin. Below the surface each of us has a different number of melanin cells, which determine whether we are dark or light in pigmentation. Generally speaking the more melanin the darker the complexion.

The Ears

The ears they do more than just hear. They give us the gift of balance telling us where we are in space at any given moment. Simply taking a step forward would be impossible without the intricate gadgetry deep inside our ears that consists of tubes filled with fluid to help keep us balanced.

The Ears have 30,000 auditory cells that transmit to the brain all kinds of sounds and different vibrations with great sensitivity.

The ear is divided into three parts: the outer ear, the middle ear and the inner ear. When we hear a sound it is reflected by the Pinna, what we usually call the ear. The sound waves then travel down the ear canal and strike the eardrum causing it to vibrate and activate the hammer, anvil, and stirrup. These are bones in the middle ear that vibrate. The sound waves then travel into the inner ear and sends signals to the brain. The brain then tells us what we are hearing.

9

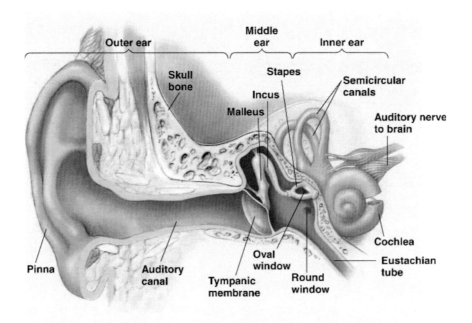

The Tongue

Our tongue has 9000 gustatory cells that sort out tastes that are sweet, sour, bitter or salty. In our throat we have vocal cords. These vocal cords vibrate to make sounds.

Breathing

A person breathes 15 breaths per minute. That's 900 breaths per hour, 21,600 breaths per day, or 7,889,400 breaths per year. Almost 8 million breaths per year. If you literally have "no time to breathe" your life could soon be over.

Blood Circulation

The Blood is pumped through your body by the heart, and it only takes 18 seconds for the blood to circulate from the heart to your toes and back up.

The Hands

Our hands consist of 25 joints and can produce 85 different types of movement. The scholars say that the hand is the most versatile moving organ on the face of the Earth. It is impossible for anyone to make a machine that can even approximate to the dexterity our hands, never mind an entire human being.

The Heart

The heart is the pump of life that never tires of working. It beats 60-80 times per minute, so it pulsates more than 100,000 times a day, pumping out 8,000 litres of blood. This is about 56 million gallons of blood in the average lifespan of a human. Is there any machine that can perform such a difficult job for such a long a time?

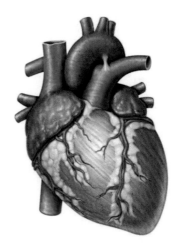

The Digestion

Before you start to eat, when you smell food, see it or even think about it, your digestion process begins, saliva begins to form in your mouth. When you eat, the food goes down your throat into the oesophagus. What this does is, it squeezes the food down to the stomach. The Stomach has three main jobs:

1. To store the food you have eaten
2. Break the food down into a liquid
3. Empty the liquid into the small intestine

The length of the small intestine is about 6 metres. Its function is to break down the food mixture even more so that your body can absorb all the vitamins, minerals, proteins, carbohydrates and fats.

The Bones

The human body has 206 bones. These bones and muscles are strong in themselves, strong enough to support up to 20 times our body weight but they are themselves very lightweight. Half of our bones are in the arms and legs.

Deep in the centre of many bones is a specialised tissue called marrow. Some 20 million oxygen-carrying red blood cells and 7 million microbe fighting white blood cells are produced there every minute and shipped off to the rest of the body.

Who created this incredible organism? Was it created by chance? All these signs show that it is Allah who created this incredible living system.

9

The Development of the Human Being

First Stage - Sperm

Allah says in the Quran that the human being is created from a (نُطْفَة - sperm), a drop, or a drop of liquid. Every bit of detailed information is in this drop. His colour, his height, his size, his shape, the colour of his eyes, everything is in this one drop.

The Quran gives detailed information about the various developmental stages:

يَٰٓأَيُّهَا ٱلنَّاسُ إِن كُنتُمْ فِى رَيْبٍ مِّنَ ٱلْبَعْثِ فَإِنَّا خَلَقْنَٰكُم مِّن تُرَابٍ ثُمَّ مِن نُّطْفَةٍ ثُمَّ مِنْ عَلَقَةٍ ثُمَّ مِن مُّضْغَةٍ مُّخَلَّقَةٍ وَغَيْرِ مُخَلَّقَةٍ لِّنُبَيِّنَ لَكُمْ وَنُقِرُّ فِى ٱلْأَرْحَامِ مَا نَشَآءُ إِلَىٰٓ أَجَلٍ مُّسَمًّى ثُمَّ نُخْرِجُكُمْ طِفْلاً

O mankind! If ye have a doubt about the Resurrection, [consider] that We created you out of dust, then out of sperm then out of a leech-like clot, then out of a morsel of flesh, partly formed and partly unformed, in order that We may manifest (Our Power) to you; and We cause whom We will to rest in the wombs for an appointed term, then do We bring you out as babes. (Quran 22:5)

Second Stage

After (نُطْفَة - sperm) the next stage is (عَلَقَة). This has three meanings. A congealed clot of blood, something that clings, and a leech-like substance. It is essential in the second stage of the (عَلَقَة) for the sperm to cling to the uterine wall, because if it does not attach to the uterine wall then the pregnancy will not continue, and a miscarriage will result.

Third Stage

The third stage is (مُضْغَة – morsel of flesh). If you look at an image of an embryo you will see that there are two parts to it: the top part, which is like a ball, and the bottom part, which is curved. One part is that from which the embryo is formed, the other part forms the placenta. In other words there is a part from which the embryo is created, and a part from which the embryo is not created. This is exactly

what the Quran says: (مُضْغَةٍ

مُخَلَّقَةٍ وَغَيْرِ مُخَلَّقَةٍ – then out [of]

a morsel of flesh, partly formed and partly unformed). Who taught Muhammad
ﷺ that there are two parts to the (مُضْغَةٍ – morsel of flesh), One part from which
the embryo is created, the head, the body, the eyes and so forth; the other part
that is not part of the embryo, which will fall away with the placenta? Who taught
Muhammad ﷺ that the morsel of flesh is partly formed and partly unformed? All
these are recent discoveries.

The Quran describes in detail the various stages of human development:

ثُمَّ خَلَقْنَا ٱلنُّطْفَةَ عَلَقَةً فَخَلَقْنَا ٱلْعَلَقَةَ مُضْغَةً فَخَلَقْنَا ٱلْمُضْغَةَ عِظَامًا فَكَسَوْنَا ٱلْعِظَامَ لَحْمًا ثُمَّ
أَنشَأْنَاهُ خَلْقًا ءَاخَرَ فَتَبَارَكَ ٱللَّهُ أَحْسَنُ ٱلْخَالِقِينَ

> Then We made the sperm into a clot of congealed blood; then of that clot
> We made a (foetus) lump; then We made out of that lump bones and
> clothed the bones with flesh; then We developed out of it another
> creature: so Blessed be Allah, the Best to create! (Quran 23:14)

The first stage of the human being in the mother's womb as we discussed above is
sperm, then it is congealed blood, then it is the foetus lump, then bones are
formed, then the bones are clothed with flesh.

The Embryo in its fifth Week

When we look at how the human being develops, we find that the eyes initially are
not formed, in the early stages there is a hollow at the place where the eyes should
be. It is the same with the ears and the mouth, there is nothing there. It is just
hollow, the openings where these parts will eventually appear. The Prophet ﷺ
said:

سجد وجهي للذي خلقه وصوره وشق سمعه وبصره

> My face fell prostrate before He who created it and he slit his faculties of
> hearing and seeing. (Narrated by Tabrani)

9

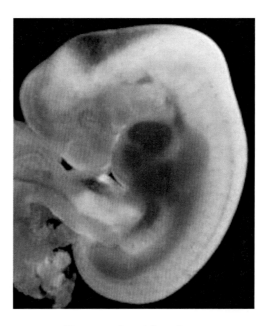

Five weeks old embryo

The Initial Stages of the Embryo of an Animal

When you look at the embryo of a human and you compare it with the embryo of any animal, whether it be a cow, fish or goat, they go through exactly the same process as the human embryo; i.e. first there is sperm, then there is congealed blood, then there is a lump, then the lump is made into bones, then the bones are clothed with flesh. To this point, it is exactly the same process for animals as for human beings. Then what does Allah say?

$$ثُمَّ أَنشَأْنَٰهُ خَلْقًا ءَاخَرَ$$

Then We developed out of it another creature: (Quran 23:14)

At this stage, it can either be a human being or an animal being created, because the initial stages are the same for both, and there is no difference. Is not The Creator One? Look at Allah's creation and glorify Him.

$$سَبِّحِ ٱسْمَ رَبِّكَ ٱلْأَعْلَى (١) ٱلَّذِى خَلَقَ فَسَوَّىٰ$$

Glorify the name of thy Guardian-Lord Most High, Who hath created, and further, given order and proportion; (Quran 87:1-2)

Who is Responsible for the Embryo?

In 1794 Kaspar Friedrich Wolff and Lazzaro Spallanzani in 1799 both said it was the male sperm that was responsible for the embryo. But Allah says:

$$يَٰٓأَيُّهَا ٱلنَّاسُ إِنَّا خَلَقْنَٰكُم مِّن ذَكَرٍ وَأُنثَىٰ$$

O mankind! We created you from a single (pair) of a male and a female (Quran 49:13)

$$إِنَّا خَلَقْنَا ٱلْإِنسَٰنَ مِن نُّطْفَةٍ أَمْشَاجٍ$$

Verily We created Man from a drop of mingled sperm (Quran 76:2)

(أَمْشَاجٍ) means a mixture of both male and female sperm.

Once, some Jews came to the Prophet ﷺ and asked him, 'From what is a human being created?' The Prophet ﷺ replied:

$$مِنْ كُلٍّ يُخْلَق مِنْ نُطْفَةِ الرَّجُل وَنُطْفَةِ الْمَرْأَة$$

With both he is created, from the sperm of man and the sperm of woman. (Musnad Ahmed)

Today science tells us that both the male sperm and the female sperm (ovum) are responsible for the embryo. Who taught Muhammad ﷺ this? It was Allah who revealed this to Muhammad ﷺ.

The Knowledge of the Unseen about Human Beings

عَنْ أَنَسِ بْنِ مَالِكٍ رَضِيَ اللَّهُ ، عَنِ النَّبِيِّ صَلَّى اللَّهُ عَلَيْهِ وَسَلَّمَ ، قَالَ " : وَكَّلَ اللَّهُ بِالرَّحِمِ مَلَكًا ، فَيَقُولُ : أَيْ رَبِّ نُطْفَةٌ ، أَيْ رَبِّ عَلَقَةٌ ، أَيْ رَبِّ مُضْغَةٌ ، فَإِذَا أَرَادَ اللَّهُ أَنْ يَقْضِيَ خَلْقَهَا ، قَالَ : أَيْ رَبِّ أَذَكَرٌ أَمْ أُنْثَى ، أَشَقِيٌّ أَمْ سَعِيدٌ ، فَمَا الرِّزْقُ ، فَمَا الْأَجَلُ ، فَيُكْتَبُ كَذَلِكَ فِي بَطْنِ أُمِّهِ

'Anas bin Malik' reported directly from Allah's Messenger ﷺ that he said: Allah, the Exalted and Glorious, has appointed an angel as the caretaker of the womb, and he would say: My Lord, it is now a drop of semen; my Lord, it is now a clot of blood; my Lord, it has now become a

9

lump of flesh, and when Allah decides to give it a final shape, the angel says: My Lord, would it be male or female or would he be an evil or a good person? What about his livelihood and his age? And it is all written as he is in the womb of his mother. (Bukhari)

This is from the knowledge of Allah and from the Unseen that only Allah knows the details of a person before he is born. The creation of a human being is a miracle. And it is not possible for someone who ponders over these signs to believe anything other than to accept that there is a Creator. Also, it is impossible that human beings are created by chance.

Leonard Nelson says, "When I looked at each and every stage of human development, from the first stage to the completion of the human being, I have to agree that behind each and every cell there is the power of Allah. The creation of the human being is amazing."

فَتَبَارَكَ ٱللَّهُ أَحْسَنُ ٱلْخَالِقِينَ

So blessed be Allah, the Best to create! (Quran 23:14)

سَنُرِيهِمْ ءَايَٰتِنَا فِى ٱلْءَافَاقِ وَفِىٓ أَنفُسِهِمْ حَتَّىٰ يَتَبَيَّنَ لَهُمْ أَنَّهُ ٱلْحَقُّ أَوَلَمْ يَكْفِ بِرَبِّكَ أَنَّهُۥ عَلَىٰ كُلِّ شَىْءٍ شَهِيدٌ

Soon will We show them Our Signs in the (furthest) regions (of the Earth), and in their own souls until it becomes manifest to them that this is the Truth. Is it not enough that thy Lord doth witness all things? (Quran 41:53)

What we have said so far about the development of the foetus and a Human is all mentioned in the Quran, look at what Allah says:

يَٰٓأَيُّهَا ٱلنَّاسُ إِن كُنتُمْ فِى رَيْبٍ مِّنَ ٱلْبَعْثِ فَإِنَّا خَلَقْنَٰكُم مِّن تُرَابٍ ثُمَّ مِن نُّطْفَةٍ ثُمَّ مِنْ عَلَقَةٍ ثُمَّ مِن مُّضْغَةٍ مُّخَلَّقَةٍ وَغَيْرِ مُخَلَّقَةٍ لِّنُبَيِّنَ لَكُمْ وَنُقِرُّ فِى ٱلْأَرْحَامِ مَا نَشَآءُ إِلَىٰٓ أَجَلٍ مُّسَمًّى ثُمَّ نُخْرِجُكُمْ طِفْلاً

O mankind! if ye have a doubt about the Resurrection, [consider] that We created you out of dust, then out of sperm then out of a leech-like clot, then out a morsel of flesh, partly formed and partly unformed, in order that We may manifest (Our Power) to you; and We cause whom We will to rest in the wombs for an appointed term, then do We bring you out as babes, (Quran 22:5)

Then Allah says:

$$\text{ثُمَّ خَلَقْنَا ٱلنُّطْفَةَ عَلَقَةً فَخَلَقْنَا ٱلْعَلَقَةَ مُضْغَةً فَخَلَقْنَا ٱلْمُضْغَةَ عِظَٰمًا فَكَسَوْنَا ٱلْعِظَٰمَ لَحْمًا ثُمَّ}$$

$$\text{أَنشَأْنَٰهُ خَلْقًا ءَاخَرَ فَتَبَارَكَ ٱللَّهُ أَحْسَنُ ٱلْخَٰلِقِينَ}$$

Then We made the sperm into a clot of congealed blood; then of that clot We made a (foetus) lump; then We made out of that lump bones and clothed the bones with flesh; then We developed out of it another creature: so blessed be Allah, the Best to create! (Quran 23:14)

Does any part of these two verses stand in contradiction to science? Are they contradicting what we have discussed about the development of the human foetus according to science? Not at all. Glory be to Allah Who has sent down the Quran. Glory be to Allah Who created human beings. O Allah, to you belongs all praises and thanks.

The Human Being was not a Thing Remembered

The verses in the Quran that talk about the creation of human beings are many, because the creation of humans is a miracle. And the Quran describes these miracles in great detail at a time when there were no special lenses or microscopes.

$$\text{خَلَقَ ٱلْإِنسَٰنَ مِن نُّطْفَةٍ فَإِذَا هُوَ خَصِيمٌ مُّبِينٌ}$$

He has created man from a sperm— drop; and behold this same [man] becomes an open disputer! (Quran 16:4)

O human being! Who are you to dispute with Allah? How can you be an atheist? Were you not a sperm? Don't you see with your eyes that you were only a sperm? Who are you to dispute the existence of Allah?

$$\text{أَوَلَمْ يَرَ ٱلْإِنسَٰنُ أَنَّا خَلَقْنَٰهُ مِن نُّطْفَةٍ فَإِذَا هُوَ خَصِيمٌ مُّبِينٌ}$$

Doth not man see that it is We Who created Him from sperm? Yet behold! He [stands forth] as an open adversary! (Quran 36:77)

$$\text{وَأَنَّهُ خَلَقَ ٱلزَّوْجَيْنِ ٱلذَّكَرَ وَٱلْأُنثَىٰ (٤٥) مِن نُّطْفَةٍ إِذَا تُمْنَىٰ}$$

9

That He did create the pairs male and female. From a sperm-drop when it is poured (into a womb) (Quran 53:45-46)

Allah is reminding us human beings to look at ourselves. We were only a sperm and yet we dispute the existence of Allah? Allah says:

$$هَلْ أَتَىٰ عَلَى ٱلْإِنسَٰنِ حِينٌ مِّنَ ٱلدَّهْرِ لَمْ يَكُن شَيْئًا مَّذْكُورًا$$

Has there not been over Man a long period of Time, when he was nothing –[not even] mentioned?– (Quran 76:1)

In other words, Allah is saying that for a long time the human being was nothing. When the human being was a sperm, he was not a thing remembered; and before sperm was he something? He was nothing worth mentioning.

$$إِنَّا هَدَيْنَٰهُ ٱلسَّبِيلَ إِمَّا شَاكِرًا وَإِمَّا كَفُورًا$$

We showed him the Way: whether he be grateful or ungrateful (Quran 76:3)

Allah has guided us on the straight path, through the knowledge of the Quran and the knowledge of science. So it is up to humans, to either be grateful or ungrateful. May Allah include us amongst His grateful servants. (Ameen)

We are Created for a Purpose

Allah has created us for a purpose, and it is not possible that this miraculous body has come into existence by chance, and without any purpose. It is not possible that humans just live this life and that's it. It is not possible. It is not possible that this miraculous creation is without a reason, without a purpose, and also it is impossible to believe that there is no wisdom behind the creation of man.

$$أَيَحْسَبُ ٱلْإِنسَٰنُ أَن يُتْرَكَ سُدًى (٣٦) أَلَمْ يَكُ نُطْفَةً مِّن مَّنِيٍّ يُمْنَىٰ (٣٧) ثُمَّ كَانَ عَلَقَةً فَخَلَقَ فَسَوَّىٰ (٣٨) فَجَعَلَ مِنْهُ ٱلزَّوْجَيْنِ ٱلذَّكَرَ وَٱلْأُنثَىٰ (٣٩) أَلَيْسَ ذَٰلِكَ بِقَٰدِرٍ عَلَىٰ أَن يُحْىِۦَ ٱلْمَوْتَىٰ$$

Does Man think that he will be left uncontrolled, [without purpose]? Was he not a drop of sperm emitted (in lowly form)? Then did he become a clinging clot; then did (Allah) make and fashion [him] in due proportion.

152

And of him He made two sexes, male and female. (Has not He, the [same] power to give life to the dead? (Quran 75:36-40)

The Minimum Length of Pregnancy

Today science tells us that the minimum length of pregnancy is 6 months. The embryo cannot live if it is less than 6 months in the womb. Once it lives for 6 months than there is a possibility that the embryo will survive. This is mentioned in the Quran where Allah says:

وَحَمْلُهُ وَفِصَالُهُ ثَلَاثُونَ شَهْرًا

The carrying [of the child] to his weaning is [a period of] thirty months. (Quran 46:15)

وَفِصَالُهُ فِى عَامَيْنِ

And his weaning is in two years. (Quran 31:14)

(فِصَالٌ) is the length of breastfeeding, which is 2 years i.e. 24 months.

(حَمْلٌ وَفِصَالٌ) i.e. pregnancy and weaning together is 30 months.

So if you calculate 30 months minus 24 months for breastfeeding, 6 months remain. This calculation is based on a pregnancy of 6 months. This tells us that, for an embryo to survive, it must be carried for a minimum of 6 months. Science today tells us that it is possible for the embryo to live if it is born only 6 months into pregnancy. Who taught Muhammad ﷺ this knowledge? It was Allah, the One Who revealed the Quran and explained this in detail for us.

Darwin's Theory

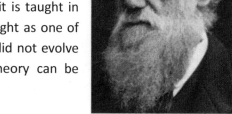

The Quran condemns Darwin's theory, and his theory is nothing more than a theory. Even when it is taught in schools, it is not taught as a fact, it is taught as one of the theories. The Quran tells us that we did not evolve from apes, our origin was dust. This theory can be

9

153

refuted in many ways, but I will just share with you one point that will persuade you that this theory is wrong.

If we were to imagine for the sake of argument that Darwin's theory is true, that we evolved from apes, then why does this process not continue? Why did it only happen that one time? If it happened once then this process should continue to happen. It happened millions of years ago: Why, then, has it not recurred? The Quran makes it very clear that humankind has been created by the hand of Allah. What would you prefer? Would you prefer to think of your great great great grandfather as an ape, or would you like to think of him as a human being? I wouldn't like to think of my great great great grandfather as an ape. The choice is yours.

The Prohibition of Pork

Amongst the miracles of Allah are the miracles of the laws that Allah revealed to us related to medicine. Medical science has advanced and told us the many illnesses a person can suffer resulting from eating pork. The scholars say that no other animal harbours as many illnesses as are found in pork. No other animal carries so many illnesses, bacteria and worms as there are in pork; and so that's the reason as to why Allah prohibited pork.

The Quran came and told the Arabs that pork is prohibited. The surprising thing is that the Arabs never used to eat Pork. Pork was not even known amongst the Arabs, but the Quran is not only for the Arabs, the Quran is guidance for the entire human race until the Day of Judgement. So Allah prohibited the flesh of swine because it is unclean, and it is shocking for a person to continue to eat the flesh of swine after becoming aware of the diseases it can cause.

The Forehead – The Seat of Thought

I would like to finish this chapter on the topic of the forehead. Allah says in the Quran:

$$ كَلَّا لَئِن لَّمْ يَنتَهِ لَنَسْفَعًا بِٱلنَّاصِيَةِ (١٥) نَاصِيَةٍ كَاذِبَةٍ خَاطِئَةٍ $$

No! If he does not desist, We will certainly drag (him) by the forelock, A lying, sinful forelock. (Quran 96:15-16)

On the Day of Judgement Allah will command the Angels to take the forehead of this disbeliever and his legs and to drag him into the Hell. But the amazing point is the particular description that the Quran gives us.

Allah did not say that the human being is a liar and sinful, Allah said that his forehead is a liar and sinful. Science today tells us that our brain has divisions, and the part from which we think and make decisions regarding truth and falsity is in the forehead. It is not the entire head that does this job. It is only the forehead that does this job and it is in this place that we choose between truth and falsehood. So when Allah said that the forehead is a liar and sinful, Allah was being concise in providing this subtlety of detail.

Summary

Today you have learnt about some of the most amazing scientific miracles in the human body that are mentioned in the Quran. You have learnt about the unlimited number of blessings that Allah has bestowed upon us. The blessing of our eyes, the blessing of our ears, the blessing of just taking one breath! Even if you were to take this one blessing and spend your entire life in prostration and thanking Allah for just one breath, even then you will never be able to thank Allah sufficiently for any one of his blessings.

There are many signs mentioned in the Quran in the field of medicine. Scholars have said that there are up to 900 signs in the Quran related to the field of medicine, and if we were to stop at every single verse in the Quran that talks about medicine, multiple volumes of a book such as this would not be sufficient. So, it was the least I could attempt to do just to open the doors for you, so that you can build for yourselves upon the knowledge that I have shared with you.

Workshop

The quiz questions and the exercises are provided to further your understanding. Don't worry if you can't answer all of the questions in the quiz. Try your best to answer as many as you can. You should go back through the chapter to check your answers to these questions.

9

Quiz 9

1. List a few of the miracles of the human body?
2. What are the stages of the human being's development in the mother's womb?
3. How does the Quran describe the minimum length of pregnancy?
4. What does the Quran tell us about the forehead?

Other Miracles Mentioned in the Quran

DAY 10

10

The Miracle of Numbers

The Miracle of Numbers is one of the most interesting miracles of the Quran, and in this section you will study miracles related to numbers, the number of times a certain word is mentioned in the Quran. When the scholars read the Quran and pondered over all the verses and reflected upon them, they discovered an amazing consistency. They discovered the following:

Arabic Word	Translation	Number of times mentioned in Quran
دنيا	World	115
اخرت	Hereafter	115
ملائكة	Angels	88
شياطين	Shaitans	88
الناس	Mankind	368
رسل	Messenger	368
ابليس	Eblees (King of Shaitans)	11
استعاذة من ابليس	Seeking refuge from Eblees	11
مصيبة	Calamity	75
شكر	Thanks	75
انفاق	Spending	73
رضاء	Satisfaction	73
ضالون	People who are misled	17
موتى	Dead people	17
مسلمين	Muslims	41
جهاد	Jihaad	41

سحر	Magic	60
فتنة	Fitnah (dissuasion, misleading)	60
زكوة	Zakah	32
بركة	Increasing or blessing of wealth	32
حياة	Life	145
موت	Death	145
عقل	Mind	49
نور	Light	49
لسان	Tongue	25
موعظة	Sermon	25
رغبة	Invitation	8
رهبة	Intimidation	8
جهر	Speaking publicly	16
علانية	Publicising	16
شدة	Hardship	114
صبر	Patience	114
محمد	Muhammed ﷺ	4
شريعة	Sharee'ah (Teachings of the Quran and Hadith)		4
رجل	Man	24
امرأة	Woman	24
صلوات	Prayers	5

شهر	Month	12
يوم	Day	365

Who taught Muhammad ﷺ to speak with this amazing accuracy and consistency? Can this consistency be accidental? Coincidence? Meaningless?

Which computer in the world can anyone use to produce such a huge book with such internal accuracy? Is this Muhammad's work ﷺ? No, never. This can be nothing other than a revelation from Allah.

Miracle of the Lunar and the Solar Calendar

Allah says in the story of the people of the cave:

$$ وَلَبِثُواْ فِى كَهْفِهِمْ ثَلَٰثَ مِائَةٍ سِنِينَ وَٱزْدَادُواْ تِسْعًا $$

They stayed in their Cave for three hundred years and added nine. (Quran 18:25)

Why didn't Allah just say 309 years instead of saying 300 and add 9 years? The scholars calculated that the solar calendar has 365 days. According to the lunar calendar there are 354 days. So if you were to multiply 365 by 300 (years) you will get the figure of 109,500. If you were to multiply 354 days by 300 (years) you will get the figure of 106,200. If you subtract the lunar days from the solar days, you will find the difference is exactly 9 years. So 300 years was the length of time according to the solar calendar, if you want to know the time according to the lunar calendar then you have to add 9 years. So the Quran is asking you, 'How do you want to work out your calculation? If You want to calculate according to the solar calendar, then it is 300 years; if you want to calculate according to the lunar calendar then it is 309 years.'

Miracle of the Percentage of Sea and Land in the World

Another of the amazing miracles of the Quran that I find is the miracle of the division of the Earth's surface between sea and land. The word (بَحْر – Sea) is mentioned 32 times in the Quran. The word (بَر – Land) is mentioned 12 times and the word (يَبَس – solidity) is mentioned once. So total number of times land is mentioned in the Quran is 13 times. If you were to add the total number of times the word sea is used in the Quran i.e. 32 times plus the number of times the word land is used, 32 + 13 = 45. If you calculate it as percentages by the number of times the word sea is used, 32/45*100 = 71.1111111%. If you calculate the land 13/45*100 = 28.88888888% (round it up: 29%). The percentage of water and land on this Earth is 71% water and 29% land.

Who calculated for Muhammad ﷺ the proportions of land and water? Who matched the number of times the words for sea and land are mentioned in the Quran to the ratio of sea and land on Earth? All these are miracles, and Allah knows best the purpose of these miracles, and there are hundreds of examples like this. Don't these miracles direct you to Allah?

When I was studying in my early years, I studied a book titled 'Maqamat Al Hariree'. It is an amazing book in terms of its style and the way it is written. In the first chapter you find that all the words are made up with letters that have dots. So in the entire chapters all the letters are those that have dots on them. Then you will come to another chapter in which all the words are without dots. It is a unique style, it has power in its language. Then you come to the third chapter, which is written using a dotted letter then a non-dotted letter. A dotted letter then a non-dotted letter. Then you come to the fourth chapter and you see that the whole

10

chapter is made up of a dotted letter then two non-dotted letters. A dotted letter then two non-dotted letters. This is an amazingly powerful language! However, when you read the book, it is very difficult to understand. Yes, the book is amazing, it is unique in its style, but the Quran is more unique and more amazing than this. In the Quran we find miracles, a unique style, unique arrangements of words, and miracles of numbers, but at the same time, there is no difficulty in understanding the Quran. Whereas when you read 'Maqamat Al Hariree' you will find it difficult to follow. The Quran is easy to read. In fact, when you read the Quran, you want to read it more and more and you don't get tired reading it. With 'Maqamat Al Hariree' you read one chapter and you get tired of it, it's too hard; you will not find this difficulty in the Book of Allah.

The Miracle of the Environment in the Quran

The Dumping of Environmentally Harmful Waste in the Sea

Allah says in the Quran:

$$ظَهَرَ ٱلْفَسَادُ فِى ٱلْبَرِّ وَٱلْبَحْرِ بِمَا كَسَبَتْ أَيْدِى ٱلنَّاسِ$$

Mischief has appeared on land and sea because of what the hands of the people have earned (Quran 30:41)

Corruption on the land, this we can understand but what does it mean by corruption in the sea? And then the verse says because of what the hands of mankind have earned? Today we know how the actions of mankind have damaged the seas due to the spillage of oil and harmful waste, all of which is being dumped by people.

The Ozone Layer in the Atmosphere

Allah says in the Quran:

$$وَجَعَلْنَا ٱلسَّمَآءَ سَقْفًا مَّحْفُوظًا$$

And We have made the Heavens as a canopy well-guarded (Quran 21:32)

Allah says that He has made the Heavens like an umbrella protecting everything beneath it. Today science tells us about 'The Ozone Layer' which was first discovered in 1913 by French physicists Charles Fabry and Henry Buisson. This layer is approximately 25 kilometres deep. If this layer was not there then the Earth would be destroyed. Is not this canopy protecting us? The scientists say that we are destroying this layer with pollution, and there are already holes in this layer. Today they are holding international conferences trying to stop the things that are affecting this Ozone Layer; to protect this layer, which protects us.

These are just some of the miracles in the Quran that I have selected to share with you related to the environment. Of course there are many more than the above-mentioned.

The Miracle of Legislation in the Quran

The laws and the legislation that the Quran has laid down for us are not only suited to the time of Muhammad ﷺ. These laws are suitable in his time, in our time and through all time until the Day of Judgement. These laws are not applicable only for the Arabs, they are for the Non-Arabs too. These laws are suitable for all times and for the whole of mankind.

Interest

Today, Interest is being taught in schools, colleges and universities as part of economics. In an interest-based system, a poor person continues to be poor and the rich person continues to be rich. If this interest-based system was replaced with the Islamic system then all the problems of economies would be solved. Of course, it may be difficult to change this interest-based system, but Islam is the solution to this problem.

Zakah

In contrast to the tax system which exists in many western countries, look at Zakah, which is one of the pillars of Islam. In the tax based system a poor person becomes

poorer and a rich person becomes richer. With Zakah, the Islamic based system, this is not the case because wealth is circulated continually and fairly, throughout society. With Zakah, you only give 2.5% of your excess wealth every lunar year to Quranically specified deserving causes.

In the taxation systems which operate in most European countries, a person who works pays tax. The more you work the larger the amount of tax that is deducted from your salary. If a person is not working because he is rich and he has a lot of savings, then there is no deduction of tax from his wealth. This is how the taxation system operates in many countries.

Let us look at what Islam has to offer. Let's look at an example taken from a Zakah based system. A person who works, who has to support his family, is not required to pay Zakah on the amount of his earnings. Instead, at the end of the lunar year, he will pay Zakah only on his savings. A rich person, who is not working but holds wealth above the *nisab* level (the amount one's net worth must exceed for the Muslim owner to become liable to give zakat.), and one whole year has passed by then he must pay Zakah every lunar year on his savings. If every rich person paid Zakah, i.e. 2.5% of excess wealth every lunar year, then poverty would be eradicated from the face of the Earth. Isn't this a fair system that Islam offers? Glory be to Allah who offered this system as a solution to the problems of poverty that plague the world today.

Law and the Solution for Criminality

Islam has given us laws and solutions for the one who steals. Once, an Oklahoma newspaper published an article stating that the Government of Oklahoma had decided to release a large number of prisoners in order to make space for other criminals in the prisons. So this is what they decided; they decided that those criminals who had committed minor crimes were to be released to make space for those criminals who had committed more serious crimes. They were asked why they didn't just build another prison. They calculated that to build one prison would cost the government of Oklahoma $30,000 annually. Who has this kind of money? They take money from the working class people, the non-criminals, and spend it on the criminals. Look at the solution the Quran has given to us. Allah says:

وَٱلسَّارِقُ وَٱلسَّارِقَةُ فَٱقْطَعُوٓاْ أَيْدِيَهُمَا جَزَآءًۢ بِمَا كَسَبَا نَكَـٰلًا مِّنَ ٱللَّهِ وَٱللَّهُ عَزِيزٌ حَكِيمٌ

As to the thief, male or female, cut off his or her hands: a retribution for their deed and exemplary punishment from Allah and Allah is Exalted in Power, full of Wisdom. (Quran 5:38)

In the first 400 years of Islamic government there were no more than 6 hands cut off <u>in 400 years</u>! If someone says that this is strict, compare this punishment with the thousands of dollars spent on – and in – prisons, and that millions of people are too afraid to walk the streets because of these thieves. Compare their solution for thieves with the solution the Quran gives for thieves.

There are many more laws and pieces of legislation that the Quran gives us which are perfect solutions for yesterday, today and till the Day of Judgement.

The Miracle of Logic in the Quran

The disbelievers once said, "How can Muhammad claim that Allah is One? How does Muhammad make all of our gods into one God?"

أَجَعَلَ ٱلْأَلِهَةَ إِلَٰهًا وَٰحِدًا إِنَّ هَٰذَا لَشَىْءٌ عُجَابٌ (٥) وَٱنطَلَقَ ٱلْمَلَأُ مِنْهُمْ أَنِ ٱمْشُوا۟ وَٱصْبِرُوا۟ عَلَىٰٓ ءَالِهَتِكُمْ إِنَّ هَٰذَا لَشَىْءٌ يُرَادُ (٦) مَا سَمِعْنَا بِهَٰذَا فِى ٱلْمِلَّةِ ٱلْءَاخِرَةِ إِنْ هَٰذَآ إِلَّا ٱخْتِلَٰقٌ

"Has he made the gods (all) into one God? Truly this is a wonderful thing!" And the leaders among them go away [impatiently], [saying] "Walk ye away, and remain constant to your gods! For this is truly a thing designed (against you)! "We never heard [the like] of this among the people of these latter days: this is nothing but a made-up tale! (Quran 38:5-7)

Muhammad ﷺ tried to remove this false belief from the unbelievers. We find this logical reply given to them in the Quran:

أَمِ ٱتَّخَذُوٓا۟ ءَالِهَةً مِّنَ ٱلْأَرْضِ هُمْ يُنشِرُونَ (٢١) لَوْ كَانَ فِيهِمَآ ءَالِهَةٌ إِلَّا ٱللَّهُ لَفَسَدَتَا فَسُبْحَٰنَ ٱللَّهِ رَبِّ ٱلْعَرْشِ عَمَّا يَصِفُونَ (٢٢) لَا يُسْئَلُ عَمَّا يَفْعَلُ وَهُمْ يُسْئَلُونَ (٢٣) أَمِ ٱتَّخَذُوا۟ مِن دُونِهِ ءَالِهَةً قُلْ هَاتُوا۟ بُرْهَٰنَكُمْ هَٰذَا ذِكْرُ مَن مَّعِىَ وَذِكْرُ مَن قَبْلِى بَلْ أَكْثَرُهُمْ لَا يَعْلَمُونَ ٱلْحَقَّ فَهُم مُّعْرِضُونَ

Or have they taken (for worship) gods from the Earth who can raise (the dead)? If there were in the Heavens and the Earth, other gods besides Allah, there would have been ruin in both! But glory to Allah the Lord of the Throne: [High is He] above what they attribute to Him! He cannot be questioned for His acts, but they will be questioned [for theirs]. Or have they taken for worship [other] gods besides Him? Say "Bring your convincing proof: this is the Message of those with me and the Message of those before me." But most of them know not the Truth and so turn away (Quran 21:21-24)

Firstly, Allah asks them to bring proof, proving that there are gods besides Allah. If you say there are other gods besides Allah, then don't just claim, bring your proof, and if you can prove it, then I (Muhammed) will agree with you and worship with you without any questions asked. Prove your gods to me and I will worship them with you.

قُلْ إِن كَانَ لِلرَّحْمَٰنِ وَلَدٌ فَأَنَا أَوَّلُ ٱلْعَٰبِدِينَ

Say: "If (Allah) Most Gracious had a son, I would be the first to worship." (Quran 43:81)

"If you prove to me that God has a son, then I will be the first to worship." The Quran instructs the disbelievers that claiming that because your forefathers did something and you want to follow them therefore you are correct; no, this is not the case: when you make claims, then you need to produce proof.

What Would Happen if There Were Gods Besides Allah

The Quran tells us in another place:

مَا ٱتَّخَذَ ٱللَّهُ مِن وَلَدٍ وَمَا كَانَ مَعَهُ مِنْ إِلَٰهٍ إِذًا لَّذَهَبَ كُلُّ إِلَٰهٍ بِمَا خَلَقَ وَلَعَلَا بَعْضُهُمْ عَلَىٰ بَعْضٍ

Allah has not taken a son to Himself, nor was there any god with Him. Had there been so, every god would have taken away what he created, and each one of them would have been aggressive against the other. (Quran 23:91)

167

10

Allah is saying that if there were many Gods and if every god was a creator then what would happen in the Heavens and on the Earth? There would be differences and arguments and conflicts. We see that in the creation of the Heavens and the Earth, there is oneness. Remember, we learnt in the previous chapters that everything in this universe and the whole universe was made from Quark?

Allah then says, fine, if there are many gods and they all agreed to create the universe, who will then run this universe? Either all the gods are equal and the same, or one of them is greater. If one of them is greater, then that one which is greater is the Supreme God and others are not God. If they are all the same and equal then what will happen? One god will say I want this person to sit, another god will say no, I want this person to stand, the third god will say no, I want this person to die. What will happen? There will either be contradictions in the universe, or one god will rule over the others: in that case the lesser ones are not gods!

Allah gives another logical reply to the disbelievers:

قُلْ أَرَءَيْتُم مَّا تَدْعُونَ مِن دُونِ ٱللَّهِ أَرُونِي مَاذَا خَلَقُوا مِنَ ٱلْأَرْضِ أَمْ لَهُمْ شِرْكٌ فِى ٱلسَّمَٰوَٰتِ ٱئْتُونِى بِكِتَٰبٍ مِّن قَبْلِ هَٰذَآ أَوْ أَثَٰرَةٍ مِّنْ عِلْمٍ إِن كُنتُمْ صَٰدِقِينَ

Say, "Tell me about those whom you invoke instead of Allah, [and] show me what they have created from the Earth; Or have they a share in [the creation of] the Heavens? Bring to me a book [revealed] before this one, or a trace of knowledge, if you are truthful." (Quran 46:4)

Allah says fine, if we agree for the sake of argument that there are gods besides Allah, then show me what have they created. Or did they share in the creation of the Heavens? Allah is saying, 'show me'. And if you cannot show then your claim does not carry any weight.

Allah is the Creator

Allah proves in the following verses that He is the Creator. Allah says:

أَمَّنْ خَلَقَ ٱلسَّمَٰوَٰتِ وَٱلْأَرْضَ وَأَنزَلَ لَكُم مِّنَ ٱلسَّمَآءِ مَآءً فَأَنۢبَتْنَا بِهِۦ حَدَآئِقَ ذَاتَ بَهْجَةٍ مَّا كَانَ لَكُمْ أَن تُنۢبِتُوا شَجَرَهَآ أَءِلَٰهٌ مَّعَ ٱللَّهِ بَلْ هُمْ قَوْمٌ يَعْدِلُونَ (٦٠) أَمَّن جَعَلَ ٱلْأَرْضَ قَرَارًا وَجَعَلَ خِلَٰلَهَآ أَنْهَٰرًا وَجَعَلَ لَهَا رَوَٰسِىَ وَجَعَلَ بَيْنَ ٱلْبَحْرَيْنِ حَاجِزًا أَءِلَٰهٌ مَّعَ ٱللَّهِ بَلْ أَكْثَرُهُمْ لَا

يَعْلَمُونَ (٦١) أَمَّن يُجِيبُ ٱلْمُضْطَرَّ إِذَا دَعَاهُ وَيَكْشِفُ ٱلسُّوءَ وَيَجْعَلُكُمْ خُلَفَاءَ ٱلْأَرْضِ أَءِلَٰهٌ

مَّعَ ٱللَّهِ قَلِيلًا مَّا تَذَكَّرُونَ

Or who has created the Heaven and the Earth, and who sends you down rain from the sky? Yea, with it We cause to grow well-planted orchards full of beauty and delight: it is not in your power to cause the growth of the trees in them. [Can there be another] god besides Allah? Nay they are a people who swerve from justice. Or, who has made the Earth firm to live in; made rivers in its midst; set thereon mountains immovable; and made a separating bar between the two bodies of flowing water? [Can there be another] god besides Allah? Nay most of them know not. Or, who listens to the [soul] distressed when it calls on Him, and who relieves its suffering, and makes you [mankind] inheritors of the Earth? [Can there be another] god besides Allah? Little it is that ye heed! (Quran 27:60-62)

When a calamity befalls someone, an earthquake, or a tsunami or a hurricane, every human being (whether a believer or not) calls upon God. I have witnessed this myself: I have not come across a single incident in my life that when a calamity has befallen a person he has said 'O Jesus', they only say 'O God'. They don't call upon anyone except God.

أَمَّن يَهْدِيكُمْ فِي ظُلُمَٰتِ ٱلْبَرِّ وَٱلْبَحْرِ وَمَن يُرْسِلُ ٱلرِّيَٰحَ بُشْرًۢا بَيْنَ يَدَىْ رَحْمَتِهِۦٓ أَءِلَٰهٌ مَّعَ ٱللَّهِ

تَعَٰلَى ٱللَّهُ عَمَّا يُشْرِكُونَ (٦٣) أَمَّن يَبْدَؤُاْ ٱلْخَلْقَ ثُمَّ يُعِيدُهُۥ وَمَن يَرْزُقُكُم مِّنَ ٱلسَّمَآءِ وَٱلْأَرْضِ

أَءِلَٰهٌ مَّعَ ٱللَّهِ قُلْ هَاتُواْ بُرْهَٰنَكُمْ إِن كُنتُمْ صَٰدِقِينَ

Or, who guides you through the depths of darkness on land and sea, and who sends the winds as heralds of glad tidings, going before His mercy? [Can there be another] god besides Allah? High is Allah above what they associate with Him! Or who originates Creation, then repeats it, and who gives you sustenance from Heaven and Earth? [Can there be another] god besides Allah? Say, "Bring forth your argument, if ye are telling the truth!" (Quran 27:63-64)

أَفَمَن يَخْلُقُ كَمَن لَّا يَخْلُقُ أَفَلَا تَذَكَّرُونَ

Is then He Who creates like one that creates not? Will ye not receive admonition? (Quran 16:17)

There are many more verses in the Quran that prove that Allah is the Creator, and He is our Lord, but mankind argues about Allah. People dispute and disagree and disbelieve. Allah says:

وَمِنَ ٱلنَّاسِ مَن يُجَٰدِلُ فِى ٱللَّهِ بِغَيْرِ عِلْمٍ وَلَا هُدًى وَلَا كِتَٰبٍ مُّنِيرٍ

Yet there is among men such a one as disputes about Allah, without knowledge, without guidance, and without a Book of Enlightenment— (Quran 22:8)

Logical Reply to Those who Deny Judgement

Allah also replies logically to those who deny the Day of Judgement. Allah says:

وَقَالَ ٱلَّذِينَ كَفَرُوا۟ هَلْ نَدُلُّكُمْ عَلَىٰ رَجُلٍ يُنَبِّئُكُمْ إِذَا مُزِّقْتُمْ كُلَّ مُمَزَّقٍ إِنَّكُمْ لَفِى خَلْقٍ جَدِيدٍ

(٧) أَفْتَرَىٰ عَلَى ٱللَّهِ كَذِبًا أَم بِهِۦ جِنَّةٌۢ بَلِ ٱلَّذِينَ لَا يُؤْمِنُونَ بِٱلْءَاخِرَةِ فِى ٱلْعَذَابِ وَٱلضَّلَٰلِ ٱلْبَعِيدِ

And the disbelievers said, "Shall we point out to you a man who informs you that, when you are totally torn into pieces, you shall be [raised] in a new creation? Has he forged a lie against Allah, or is there a sort of madness in him?" No, but those who do not believe in the Hereafter are in torment and far astray from the right path. (Quran 34:7-8)

In reply to this, in another verse of the Quran, Allah says:

أَفَعَيِينَا بِٱلْخَلْقِ ٱلْأَوَّلِ بَلْ هُمْ فِى لَبْسٍ مِّنْ خَلْقٍ جَدِيدٍ

Were We then weary with the first Creation, that they should be in confused doubt about a new Creation? (Quran 50:15)

Creating something for the first time is more difficult than recreating.' So Allah is saying that He created you the first time, (which is supposed to be difficult, but of course for Allah it is not) how can it be difficult for Allah to create you for the second time? A clear and logical response from Allah.

Allah repeats the same point in Surah Yaseen:

وَضَرَبَ لَنَا مَثَلاً وَنَسِيَ خَلْقَهُ قَالَ مَن يُحْيِ ٱلْعِظَمَ وَهِيَ رَمِيمٌ (٧٨) قُلْ يُحْيِيهَا ٱلَّذِىٓ أَنشَأَهَآ أَوَّلَ مَرَّةٍ وَهُوَ بِكُلِّ خَلْقٍ عَلِيمٌ

And he makes comparisons for us, and forgets his own [Origin and] Creation: He says "Who can give life to [dry] bones and decomposed ones [at that]?" Say "He will give them life Who created them for the first time! For He is well-versed in every kind of creation!– (Quran 36:78-79)

There are many other verses in the Quran in which Allah replies logically to the disbelievers.

Summary

Today was your last day of this 10 day course, and we dedicated today's lesson to some of the other miracles that Allah talks about in the Quran. Today you learnt the miracles of numbers in the Quran, and you learnt the miracles related to the environment. Finally, you learnt about the miracle of logic in the Quran, how the Quran uses logic to prove about Allah to the disbelievers.

Workshop

The quiz questions and the exercises are provided to further your understanding. Don't worry if you can't answer all of the questions in the quiz. Try your best to answer as many as you can. You should go back through the chapter to check your answers to these questions.

Quiz 10

1. What are some of the Miracle of Numbers in the Quran?
2. When Allah tells the story of the people in the cave, why does He say that they stayed in their cave for three hundred years and add nine?
3. What is the magnificence of Zakah in contrast to the tax based system?

Conclusion

This book, which is about the miracles in the Quran, contains only a few of the miracles to be found in the Quran. So, the Quran does not only contain the ones we have studied; there are thousands more miracles in the Quran. However, my intention is to open up the doors for you so that you reflect on these miracles, and then you can go further into other miracles not discussed in this book and thereby increase your Iman.

The second thing I want from you, is to change your approach with the recitation of the Quran. The recitation of Quran is not simply about getting through the Quran just to finish, to get to the end. I hope that your recitation will now change into a recitation of reflection and pondering over the verses, and increasing your Iman by recognising the miracles in the Book of Allah.

I also hope that this course will be a means for you to increase your Iman. Not that you have no Iman, you undoubtedly have some Iman, but it needs to increase in order to satisfy your heart. Prophet Ibrahim ﷺ asked Allah, "How will you give life to the dead?" Allah asked in return, "Don't you have Iman? Don't you believe?" Ibrahim ﷺ replied, "Yes, O Allah, I do believe, but I want peace of mind." So when Ibrahim ﷺ wants peace of mind, then don't you think that you and I want the same?

Also remember that there are no contradictions between the Quran and proven scientific facts because the One who revealed the Quran is the One who created the universe.

These miracles will, if Allah wills, also become a means to stop you from disobeying Allah. For how can you disobey Allah when you see His power in His creation and in this universe?

Finally, I am a human being and I can make mistakes. If anything that I have written is correct it is from Allah, and if anything that I written is incorrect then it is from myself and from the Shaitan.

O Allah! The one who sent this book (Quran), light our hearts with the Quran and make the Quran the light of our soul and the relief of our sorrows and griefs, and guide us to the straight path

O Allah! Help us to recite the Quran all day and night in the way that pleases You. O Allah! Let it be a cure for our hearts and a remedy for our diseases and let it be our saviour from the Hell Fire.

O Allah! Let us be amongst the people of the Quran and amongst those who are the closest to You.

O Allah! Let us be of those who do the Halaal things mentioned in the Quran and avoid the Haraam things mentioned in it. Let us be of those who recite it well and understand its clear meanings, as well as the hidden ones.

O Allah! Make victorious Your religion, Your Book (the Quran), and the Sunnah of the Prophet Muhammad ﷺ.

O Allah! Take us closer towards Your pleasure, and keep us away from Your anger and punishment. Grant us the opportunity to recite Your verses (of the Quran), by Your Mercy.

Ameen.

S. Sirajudin.

Suhaib Sirajudin

Bolton

15th November 2015

Bibliography

Bownet.org (1996) Three Types of Clouds, [Online] Available from: http://www.bownet.org/sbennert/Three%20Main%20Types%20of%20Clouds.htm (Last Accessed on 8th November 2014)

Harun Yahya (2008) Miracles of the Quran, Al-Attique Publishers.

Mission Islam (n.d) The Scientific Miracles of the Qur'an, [Online] Available from: http://www.missionislam.com/science/book.htm (Last Accessed on 13th November 2014)

Pilates 4 Me, (2014) The Human Body, [Online] Available from: http://pilates4.me/human-body/ (Last Accessed on 2nd November 2014)

T Sowaydan (n.d) I'Jazul Quran [CD-ROM] Qurtobah.

Way to Allah, Oceanology [Online] Available from: http://www.way-to-allah.com/en/miracles/oceanology.html (Last Accessed on 15th October 2014)

Yusuf Al-Hajj Ahmad (2010) Scientific wonders on the earth and in space, Darussalam.

Yusuf Al-Hajj Ahmad (2010) The Unchallengeable Miracles of the Quran, Darussalam.

Zakir Naik, Qur'an and Modern Science: Compatible or Incompatible? [Online] Available from: http://Sunnahonline.com/library/the-majestic-quran/430-quran-and-modern-science-compatible-or-incompatible-the#h13-1-i-man-is-created-from-alaq-a-leech-like-substance (Last Accessed on 20th October)

Appendixes

A Answers

B Using the Website

APPENDIX **A**

Answers

Quiz 1

1. A miracle is an impossibility, something beyond human capacity.
2. First difference, the Quran is a challenge to every human being unlike the other miracles.

    Second difference, the Quran is an aural miracle, unlike other miracles they were visual.

    Thrid difference, the Quran is not time-bound neither it is place-bound unlike other miracles.

    Fourth difference, the Quran is two in one, a message and a miracle together which was not the case with other miracles.
3. First reason, Quran is a miracles until the Day of Judgement.

    Second reason, the disbelievers would yet not believe if the Prophet was given miracles other than the Quran.

    Third reason, all other miracles were small compared to the Quran.

    Fourth reason was the mercy of Allah being granted to the disbelievers.
4. First Proof, Prophet told the companions not to mix the Quran with the Hadith

    Second Proof, Many instances occured where by if the revelation came down at a specific time it would have benefited the Prophet.

    Third Proof, Many verses came questioning Muhammed ﷺ
5. The story of Umar (R.A), his acceptance of Islam upon reciting the first few verses of Surah Ta-Ha

Quiz 2

1. The demand of the Quraish was that the Quran if it is revealed to either Waleed Ibn Mughayrah or Urwah Ibn Masood they will accept Islam.
2. The stetement of Waleed when he gathered the people during Hajj season, he said: "By God! The words spoken by this person resemble none of these. By God! It is very pleasant and lively. Its branches are laden with fruit. Its roots are well watered. It will definitely dominate and nothing will be able to dominate it, and it will crush everything below it."
3. Abu Sufyan, Akhnas ibn Shurayh and Abu Jahl left their homes in the last part of the night, stealthily, to listen to the recitation of the Quran.
4. He accepted Islam upon hearing the Quran.
5. To find one single mistake in the Quran.
6. Islam will Prevail over all other Religions and Muslims will be Victorious
7. This change is due to a change in the subject.
8. They failed to match the Quran's message, guidance, style and eloquence.

Quiz 3

1. The whole Quran is a miracle.
2. In (Quran 25:30) Allah used the word (مَهْجُورًا) and not (مَتْرُوْكًا), because (مَتْرُوْكًا) means to leave something but (مَهْجُورًا) means to leave something far behind.
3. This is because there are two types of relationship. The first type is based on religion and the second type is based on children.
4. A sin is when a person derives pleasure from committing it and injustice to a soul is a sin without pleasure.
5. (يُوَسْوِسُ) Repetition in a letter indicates repetition in an action.
6. To tell us that the future will come with so much certainty that there can be no doubt about it.

Quiz 4

1. The Surah are in such an order that there is a link between each Surah. It was the way Allah wanted for this order to be the way it is now.

2. (Quran 6:151) refers to the one who is poor whilst (Quran 17:31) refers to the one who is not poor.
The reversed order between (Quran 2:173) and (Quran 15:49). This is because knowledge requires mercy from Allah.
3. (Quran 41:30) One word contains the entire meaning of obedience to Allah. (Quran 5:1) One word contains all kind of contracts.

Quiz 5

1 They will not enter Paradise until a camel passes through the eye of a needle.
2 Allah will make the deeds of the non-believers as floating dust scattered about.
3 Allah describes him as a dog: if you attack him, he lolls out his tongue or if you leave him alone, he (still) lolls out his tongue.

Quiz 6

1 1) Quran is a book of guidance 2) Quran has different topics to quench your thirst.
2 The existence of gravity is referred to the heavens with pillars mentioned in the Quran.
3 The heavens and the earth were joined together and Allah clove then asunder.
4 The theory of 'The Big Crunch' is similar to the description of the Quran, how the universe will come to an end.

Quiz 7

1 The light of the Sun is its own light whereas the light of the Moon is reflected (or borrowed) light.
2 Both the Sun and the Moon have temperatures, sizes, and distances accurately established with respect to the Earth.
3 There are certain stars that revolve around two easts and two wests.
4 This is a distinct environment that is created when the water of the sea mixes with the water of the river.

Quiz 8

1   At a depth of 10 meters, the red light disappears. Orange rays are absorbed at 30 to 50 metres, yellow at 50 to 100 metres, green at 100 to 200 metres, and finally, blue beyond 200 metres and so on.

2   The Quran talks about the three main types of clouds; Cumulus, Cirrus and Tornadoes. Quran besides mentioning them, also gives a description of each type of cloud.

3   Quran describes mountains as pegs and standing firm.

4   The lowest point on earth is The Dead Sea. (Quran 30:1-4)

Quiz 9

1   The eyes that Allah has given to us, 90% of the information that a human being gets is through the eyes. The skin that Allah has given to us, in one square inch of skin there are 625 sweat glands and 90 oil glands. The ears besides hearing they also give us the gift of balance.

2   The first stage is sperm, the second stage is congealed clot of blood, the third stage is morsel of flesh, the fourth stage is bones and the fifth stage is clothing the bones with flesh.

3   The length of breastfeeding is 24 months, and pregnancy and weaning together is 30 months. This shows that the minimum length of pregnancy is 6 months.

4   Forehead is the place by which we think and make decisions regarding truth and falsity.

Quiz 10

1.   The word 'World' and 'Hereafter' are mentioned 115 times in the Quran
The word 'Angels' and 'Shaitans' are mentioned 88 times in the Quran
The word 'Mankind' and 'Messenger' are mentioned 368 times in the Quran
The word 'Calamity' and 'Thanks' are mentioned 75 times in the Quran

2.   This is based on the Solar and the Lunar Calendar.

3.   In a tax based system, a rich person becomes richer and a poor person becomes poorer. In a Zakah based system, the wealth is distributed fairly amongst the people.

APPENDIX **B**

Using the Website

Website Instructions

1. Logon to www.suhaibsirajudin.com

2. Select courses and Training from the menu.

3. Click on 'Access Material' under 'Miracles of the Quran' section.

4. Put in your code: **[47240]** and you will get access to all the PowerPoint Presentations for each chapter of this course.